HARVARD POLITICAL STUDIES

PUBLISHED UNDER THE DIRECTION OF THE
DEPARTMENT OF GOVERNMENT IN
HARVARD UNIVERSITY

HARVARD POLITICAL STUDIES

A BRIEF HISTORY OF THE CONSTITUTION AND GOVERNMENT
OF MASSACHUSETTS
By Louis Adams Frothingham

THE POLITICAL WORKS OF JAMES I
Edited by Charles Howard McIlwain

POLITICA METHODICE DIGESTA OF JOHANNES ALTHUSIUS
Edited by Carl Joachim Friedrich

MUNICIPAL CHARTERS
By Nathan Matthews

A BIBLIOGRAPHY OF MUNICIPAL GOVERNMENT
By William Bennett Munro

TOWN GOVERNMENT IN MASSACHUSETTS 1630–1930
By John F. Sly

INTERSTATE TRANSMISSION OF ELECTRIC POWER
By Hugh Langdon Elsbree

AMERICAN INTERPRETATIONS OF NATURAL LAW
By Benjamin Fletcher Wright, Jr.

SANCTIONS AND TREATY ENFORCEMENT
By Payson Sibley Wild, Jr.

FOREIGN RELATIONS IN BRITISH LABOUR POLITICS
By William Percy Maddox

ADMINISTRATION OF THE CIVIL SERVICE IN MASSACHUSETTS
By George C. S. Benson

INTERNATIONAL SOCIALISM AND THE WORLD WAR
By Merle Fainsod

THE PRESIDENT'S CONTROL OF THE TARIFF
By John Day Larkin

FEDERAL COMMISSIONERS
By E. Pendleton Herring

GOVERNMENT PROPRIETARY CORPORATIONS IN THE
ENGLISH-SPEAKING COUNTRIES
By John Thurston

THE PHYSIOCRATIC DOCTRINE OF JUDICIAL CONTROL
By Mario Einaudi

THE PHYSIOCRATIC DOCTRINE
OF JUDICIAL CONTROL

———

PUBLISHED WITH THE AID OF THE
LOUIS ADAMS FROTHINGHAM FUND

LONDON : HUMPHREY MILFORD

OXFORD UNIVERSITY PRESS

The Physiocratic Doctrine of Judicial Control

BY

MARIO EINAUDI

WITH AN INTRODUCTION BY
CHARLES HOWARD McILWAIN

CAMBRIDGE, MASSACHUSETTS
HARVARD UNIVERSITY PRESS
1938

PRINTED AT THE HARVARD UNIVERSITY PRESS

CAMBRIDGE, MASS., U.S.A.

To

MY FATHER

FOREWORD

LESS attention has been given to the political aspect of the theories of the physiocrats than to their economic views. In this little book Dr. Einaudi explains and shows the importance of one element in their political thought, their doctrine — or the doctrine of some of them — of judicial review as an indispensable safeguard of the rights of individuals in a state.

Dr. Einaudi does not assert, in fact, he denies that these theories as stated by the physiocrats had any actual influence on the later development of similar views in the United States. In this he is probably correct; but the fundamental importance of his doctrine at the center of our constitutional system, and the present controversies concerning it emphasize the need and the timeliness of a study which treats of these significant principles wherever and whenever they are found. On the other hand, it seems curious that Dupont, the one important member of the physiocratic school to come to America, put less emphasis on judicial review than most others and seems never to have referred to it after he came to the United States.

In eighteenth-century France, as Dr. Einaudi shows in one of the most interesting parts of his book, the abstract idea of judicial review as a means of ensuring the permanence of the fundamentals of the physiocratic doctrine was probably in part an outcome of the Parliament of Paris and of the theory that a royal ordinance must be registered by the Parliament if it was to be binding. While this is true, Dr. Einaudi makes it equally clear that it applies only to the abstract notion of judicial review, not to the concrete institution of the Parliament. To men opposed to absolutism, as the physiocrats were, the king's frequent practice of overriding in a *lit de justice* the constitutional objections of his Parliament rendered that historic institution wholly inadequate as a safeguard of natural rights against arbitrary government.

The most interesting aspect of Dr. Einaudi's study, viewed as a whole, is the close if not inevitable relation it discloses in any system of fixed and permanent principles to some kind of judicial interpretation. The principles which the physiocrats assumed to be "natural," and therefore immutable, may be totally different from the fundamentals of our own constitutional system, but it is interesting to find men at such a different time holding that fundamentals of any kind imply a judicial interpretation which in defining them thereby sets limits to governmental will.

The current prominence of this question in the United States makes very timely this study of physiocratic doctrine in one of its aspects which is no less essential because it has received slighter attention than others.

CHARLES H. MCILWAIN

CONTENTS

I. INTRODUCTION 3

II. THE PHYSIOCRATIC "DISCOVERY" 10

III. THE PHYSIOCRATIC SOURCES OF THE DOCTRINE OF JUDICIAL
    CONTROL 13

IV. THE PHYSIOCRATIC CONCEPT OF NATURAL ORDER 20

V. THE MEANS FOR THE REALIZATION OF THE NATURAL ORDER OF
    PHYSIOCRACY 27
    1. Legal Despotism 27
    2. Judicial Control 29

VI. WAYS AND LIMITS OF JUDICIAL CONTROL 47
    1. The Precedent of Parliament 47
    2. The Constitutional Place of Judicial Control According
       to Le Mercier 53
    3. Dupont and His Abandonment of Judicial Control . . 59

VII. THE RECEPTION IN FRANCE OF THE PHYSIOCRATIC DOCTRINE OF
    JUDICIAL CONTROL 66
    1. The School and the Doctrine 66
    2. The Contemporary Critics 69

VIII. PHYSIOCRACY AND AMERICA 73
    1. Independence and the Constitution 73
    2. The Issue of Judicial Review. Stevens versus Adams 81
    3. Jefferson and Dupont 83
    4. The American and Physiocratic Doctrines of Judicial
       Control 87

INDEX 91

THE PHYSIOCRATIC DOCTRINE OF
JUDICIAL CONTROL

CHAPTER I

INTRODUCTION

THE political doctrines of the physiocrats, no less than their economic doctrines, have fared poorly at the hands of their enemies and friends alike. Excessive praise and excessive blame have been piled upon the heads of the philosopher-economists. While on the one hand they have been alternately hailed as the founders of political economy and as the most obscure and confused set of writers who ever touched economic problems, on the other hand their political theories have been called individualistic, socialistic, revolutionary, and reactionary. Thus, in discussing the physiocrats as anticipators of the Revolution, Tocqueville ascribes to the school an utter contempt of all institutions of the past, together with a belief that "there are no longer private rights, but only a common utility." [1] Baudeau's words, "The State molds men to its liking," are for Tocqueville a true summary of the physiocratic political doctrine, leading to the most fearful form of democratic despotism. Indeed, the centralizing process has been pushed so far by the physiocrats, that a socialist state is the inevitable conclusion, since "centralization and socialism spring from the same soil." [2] Their doctrine, adds another commentator, "was easily convertible into a revolutionary doctrine. The 'right of man to the things proper to his enjoyment' was not . . . easily distinguished from the 'right to live,' to which the Abbé Raynal appealed, or the 'right to labor' invoked by other popular leaders at a later date." [3] Others, however, not only have denied any revolutionary implication in the physiocratic doctrine, but have asserted (a) that an undiluted absolute monarchy is the true physiocratic state; [4] or (b) that "the theory of legal despotism which is the basis of the political principles of the school is nothing but a theoretical justifica-

---

[1] Alexis Clérel de Tocqueville, *Ancien régime* (4th ed.; Paris, 1860), p. 257.

[2] *Ibid.*, p. 265.

[3] James Bonar, *Philosophy and Political Economy* (3d ed.; London, 1922), pp. 44–45.

[4] Otto Gierke, *Natural Law and the Theory of Society, 1500–1800*, ed. Ernest Barker (Cambridge, 1934), II, 336; Henry Michel, *L'Idée de l'état* (Paris, 1896), p. 22.

tion of the status quo"; [5] or (c) that the defense of individual rights is their starting point and the defense of property rights their sole aim.[6] From such extreme positions a few writers have attempted to extricate themselves. Thus Cheinisse, in the best existing essay on the political doctrines of the physiocrats, takes Tocqueville to task for his collectivistic interpretation; [7] and to those individualists à outrance who had made of the physiocrats their champions Oncken recalls the existence of Le Trosne's De l'ordre social to prove that the interests of the state had not been forgotten.[8]

If any one particular cause can be found to explain these widely differing interpretations, it is in the misunderstanding which arose out of the two words legal despotism. Legal despotism has been commonly held to be the pivot on which the whole political doctrine of the school turns. This would be entirely proper if the complementary problem of the guarantees devised to accompany the system of legal despotism were kept in mind at the same time. The fact indeed can hardly be overstressed that the guarantees brought forward by the physiocrats to keep the legal despot within certain clearly defined limits are an integral and essential part of their system. What happened, however, was that the guarantees were practically never so considered. Either the importance of one guarantee was unduly emphasized at the expense of another, or the very existence of guarantees was forgotten entirely. If remembered at all, it was when the theories of the school had already been appraised in terms of a system of legal despotism alone. Such an interpretation inevitably destroyed whatever value might later be grudgingly accorded the system of guarantees.

The existence of certain inviolable natural law principles was the foundation upon which the physiocrats built their system of guarantees. But it is not enough merely to acknowledge this fact, as Oncken does in his highly interesting study of the school,[9] with-

[5] René Girard, "Le mouvement physiocratique," Revue de synthèse historique (October, 1912), p. 206.
[6] G. Schelle, "Physiocrates," Nouveau Dictionnaire d'économie politique (Paris, 1891–92), II, 483; G. Weulersse, Le Mouvement physiocratique en France (1756–1770) (Paris, 1910), II, 688.
[7] Léon Cheinisse, Les Idées politiques des physiocrates (Paris, 1914), pp. 57, 86. The same criticism of Tocqueville's interpretation was advanced by Léonce de Lavergne, Les Économistes français du XVIIIe siècle (Paris, 1870), p. 216.
[8] August Oncken, Geschichte der Nationaloekonomie (Leipzig, 1902), pp. 352–353.
[9] Ibid., p. 353.

out inquiring further concerning the weapons provided to secure the despots' respect for these natural law principles. This is particularly so in the face of the strong evidence that Quesnay and his followers did not erect a defenseless bulwark against the whims of the ruler, but did all they could to provide it with weapons.

The greatest variety of opinion exists concerning the exact nature of the weapons which were to secure the triumph of natural laws. If any attempt at classification is to be made, we must place first those critics who see as the only defense allowed by the physiocrats a public opinion made fully conscious of its duties by the universal teaching of the doctrines of the school. "The only guarantee contrived by the physiocrats against the abuse of power is public education," writes Tocqueville,[10] and Lavergne, on this point in full agreement with Tocqueville, is even more emphatic. The ruler must limit himself to the execution of natural laws: "if he goes beyond, he will meet an invincible opposition, not in particular bodies, not in assemblies or corporations, which always presuppose the existence of privileges, but in the whole nation, enlightened to perfection of its duties and of its rights." [11] Both Tocqueville and Lavergne were of course right in stressing the significance of the role played by public education and by public opinion in the physiocratic scheme of things. Whoever has read Le Trosne's *De l'ordre social* has admired the passionate pages on the argument, and no member of the school has failed to emphasize the importance of an educated nation alive to its responsibilities. But it is a narrow interpretation which limits itself to this particular point, and an even narrower one which grants natural laws in the physiocratic system no other sanctions than the self-interest and the benevolence of the despot.[12] Upon this view Schelle improves a little by admitting for the first time, besides the enlightened self-interest of the sovereign, the existence of "a kind of judicial power, both to administer justice and to verify the compatibility of the sovereign's orders with natural laws." [13] But without inquiring further into the matter, Schelle hastens to condemn the scheme as sophistic and contra-

---

[10] Tocqueville, *Ancien régime*, p. 258.

[11] Lavergne, *Les Économistes*, p. 72.

[12] André Blondel, *Le Contrôle juridictionnel de la constitutionnalité des lois* (Aix-en-Provence, 1927), p. 290. See, however, p. 292 for a contradictory elaboration of this point.

[13] Gustave Schelle, *Du Pont de Nemours* (Paris, 1888), p. 90. Before Schelle, Janet had made a very brief, and disparaging, reference to the judicial guarantee (*Histoire de la science politique* [4th ed.; Paris, 1913], II, 644).

dictory to the system of legal despotism,[14] a belief shared to some extent by Weulersse in his very elaborate treatise on the physiocrats.[15] Weulersse's treatment of the entire problem of the guarantees is not free from contradictions; for having at first enlarged upon the traditional view by admitting the triple guarantee of judges, education, and self-interest,[16] he appears to agree later with those unknown critics who find in the force of "evidence" the only defense against the sovereign.[17] By considering the guarantees an extraneous matter to be treated only incidentally, Weulersse was obviously laboring under the same misunderstanding which had hitherto prevented a satisfactory discussion of their nature and of their interrelation with the system of legal despotism.

This conception is happily abandoned by Cheinisse, who for the first time makes the problem of guarantees an integral part of physiocratic political doctrines and gives a more complete and logical picture of it than had been customary before. According to Cheinisse, the traditional conception of the physiocratic state as a tyrannical state is wrong: "To maintain that the physiocrats had no respect for individual rights and did not recognize any limit to the state's authority is no more correct than to attribute to them a purely negative conception of the state's duties." [18] Nor is it true, he adds, that knowledge of the principles of natural law by the public is the only defense against the state. If that was the premise from which the physiocrats started, it was not their last word on the matter. They also insisted upon the creation of a permanent and numerous crown council, without which, in Quesnay's words, monarchy "ne peut être qu'une folle le glaive à la main." [19] It is true that this body had merely advisory and consultative functions and that it could not undertake to oppose and resist the sovereign's will. But precisely because they felt the necessity of a positive and firm control upon the sovereign legislative power, the physiocrats crowned their system of guarantees by entrusting to the judicial body the ultimate power of passing upon all legislative acts to test their compatibility with the principles of natural law. "Through the magistrates public opinion will be able to assert it-

[14] Schelle, *Du Pont*, pp. 91–92.
[15] Weulersse, *Le Mouvement physiocratique*, II, 63.
[16] *Ibid.*, pp. 62–71.
[17] *Ibid.*, pp. 658–659.
[18] *Les Idées politiques*, p. 86.
[19] Cf. below, p. 29.

self most efficaciously." [20] One cannot but agree with Cheinisse in thus giving to judicial control the highest place in the system of guarantees devised by the physiocrats for the proper carrying out of their scheme of government.

As the title implies, the present monograph will be entirely dedicated to a study of the judicial guarantee, the author's interest in the matter having been prompted both by a realization of its great importance for a proper understanding of physiocratic thought and by dissatisfaction with the inadequacy of its previous treatment.

The existence of a physiocratic doctrine of judicial control, was quietly forgotten until the end of the nineteenth century. We find no reference whatever to it in Kellner,[21] Baudrillart,[22] Tocqueville, Lavergne, Hasbach,[23] Bonar, Michel, or Oncken. Schelle, as we have already seen, is the first to discuss the issue of judicial control, but he does so very casually and without giving it any importance. Weulersse closes his work with a bitter criticism of the alleged physiocratic system of guarantees, and in judicial control is unable to see anything more important than "the absurd pretense of consecrating parliaments as the representatives of the nation." [24] Both Schelle and Weulersse dismiss the theory of judicial control as incompatible with the doctrine of legal despotism. The same casual treatment is to be found in a number of other writers.[25] The first to touch briefly upon the doctrine of judicial control as the concluding link of a chain of principles rationally constructed was Léon Ameline,[26] followed, as already seen, by Cheinisse, whose

[20] Cheinisse, Les Idées politiques, p. 115.

[21] G. Kellner, Zur Geschichte des Physiocratismus (Goettingen, 1847).

[22] H. Baudrillart, "La Philosophie des Physiocrates," Journal des économistes, XXIX (1851), 1–17 (reprinted in Études de philosophie morale et d'économie politique, II [Paris, 1858], 501–529).

[23] W. Hasbach, "Les Fondements philosophiques de l'économie politique de Quesnay et de Smith," Revue d'économie politique, II (1893), 747–795).

[24] Weulersse, Le Mouvement physiocratique, II, 733. For a better appreciation of the judicial guarantee on Weulersse's part, see his article "Le Mercier de la Rivière," in Encyclopaedia of the Social Sciences, X, 353.

[25] For instance, H. Higgs, The Physiocrats (London, 1897), p. 71; Lotte Silberstein, Le Mercier de la Rivière und seine politischen Ideen (Berlin, 1928), p. 52; Wolfgang Petzet, Der Physiocratismus und die Entstehung des wirtschaftlichen Kreislaufes (Karlsruhe, 1929), p. 38.

[26] Léon Ameline, L'Idée de la souveraineté d'après les écrivains français du XVIIIe siècle (Paris, 1904), pp. 286–287.

contribution is of far greater significance.[27] Even if the relative weight given to our problem in the economy of physiocratic thought has thus been notably increased by more recent contributions, one still finds neither improved understanding in its interpretation nor, more important still, greater knowledge of the real extent to which the physiocratic school identified itself with the doctrine of judicial control. Commentators either compare the physiocratic judges to the Supreme Court of the United States or, more frequently, trace the derivation of their duties of control from the allegedly similar powers enjoyed since time immemorial by the French *parlements*. Thus Schelle speaks of "a sovereign court, similar to that created in the United States," [28] and Ameline writes of

an institution similar to that which was to become the Supreme Court of the United States. . . . One is aware of the excellent results . . . of this essential part of the American constitutional machinery. The Supreme Court is indeed an efficient guarantee of integral respect for the declaration of the rights of men. It prevents their arbitrary violation by the community; while in France the declaration of rights of 1789 is without sanction.[29]

But these rather facile comparisons, not backed by a clear understanding of the working of the American Court,[30] were not acceptable to a majority of writers, who thought a more obvious explanation lay in the traditions of the French parliaments. Such is Güntzberg's opinion,[31] and such is also in substance Weulersse's, who finds a great similarity between the *droit de remontrance* of the parliaments and the control which was to be exercised by the physiocratic judges. Weulersse, however, does not inquire into the respective validity, in theory, of a *remontrance* by parliament and of an opinion by the judges, and merely suggests that the physiocrats were bent upon winning the favor of the various parliaments in order to facilitate the acceptance of their economic reforms.[32] Nor does Cheinisse go beyond a brief acceptance of this interpretation.[33]

[27] Cf. also, for a more satisfactory discussion, B. Güntzberg, *Die Gesellschafts- und Staatslehre der Physiokraten* (Leipzig, 1907), pp. 109ff.; André Lorion, *Les Théories politiques des premiers Physiocrates* (Paris, 1918), pp. 114–119, 157.

[28] Schelle, "Physiocrates," *Nouveau Dictionnaire d'économie politique*, II, 484.

[29] Ameline, *L'Idée de la souveraineté*, p. 287.

[30] Cf. especially Lorion, *Les Théories politiques*, p. 118.

[31] Güntzberg, *Die Gesellschafts- und Staatslehre der Physiokraten*, p. 109.

[32] Weulersse, *Le Mouvement physiocratique*, II, 63–64. Weulersse suggests that Esmein (*La Science politique des physiocrates*) compared the constitutional jurisdiction of the physiocratic judges with that of the American Supreme Court. This does not appear to be correct, since nowhere does Esmein refer to this argument.

[33] Cheinisse, *Les Idées politiques*, p. 118. Cf. also Petzet, *Der Physiocratismus*, p. 38.

As for the extent to which the physiocratic system identified itself with judicial control, Weulersse's statement that "La Rivière and Dupont are the only physiocrats to grant the judicial power a political and constitutional jurisdiction," [34] has been universally held as the final word on the matter. The development of Dupont's thought has not been traced, the significance of Le Mercier's later writings has not been sufficiently emphasized, and the works of other members of the school have not been examined. This is, indeed, not to be wondered at, since, as we have seen, the entire problem of guarantees has been relegated to a secondary place.

A more complete and careful examination of the sources seemed to indicate the desirability of a new study of the whole matter in an attempt to clear up the contradictions and to fill the lacunae briefly indicated in this introduction. For in the course of the examination it soon became apparent that the doctrine of judicial control had had a much greater importance in the physiocratic system and had been much more widely held than has been commonly assumed.

A brief preliminary discussion of the economic "discovery" of the physiocrats and a description of the principal sources of the physiocratic doctrine of judicial control precede the central part of the essay. This portion concerns itself, first, with the concept of natural order held by the physiocrats; second, with a description of the steps leading to the doctrine of guarantees and of the means provided for the realization of the order; third, with the form and scope of judicial control. A brief summary of the reception accorded the doctrines of the school in France follows. The essay concludes with a survey of the relations between the physiocratic school and America, which will throw additional light on our problem, and with a comparison of the physiocratic and American doctrines of judicial control.

[34] Weulersse, *Le Mouvement physiocratique*, II, 64.

CHAPTER II

THE PHYSIOCRATIC "DISCOVERY"

THE economic discovery of Quesnay which led to the formation of the physiocratic school was the basis of the political system expounded by Quesnay himself in its essence, and by his followers in greater detail. The doctrine of legal despotism must be viewed as a consequence of the *Tableau économique*. The prince was the instrument used by the physiocrats for carrying out their program of economic reform. And the system of guarantees was devised as a control upon the actions of the prince. These three aspects of physiocratic thought must all be kept in mind, and they must be viewed as a logical sequence. Thus one would miss completely the significance of legal despotism if one considered it apart from the economic program which alone justified it and from the guarantees which on all sides checked it, since no despotism was sanctioned by the physiocrats for its own sake. One would fail likewise to give judicial control its due place, if one considered it merely as a contradictory attempt to stay the hand of a prince previously endowed with unlimited powers, instead of as the logical conclusion of a doctrine, not attempting to set up an absolute government, but bent upon introducing radical changes in the economic system and upon making the judges ultimately responsible for the success of the enterprise.

The economic aspect of the physiocratic doctrine is indeed the key which opens the door to a correct interpretation of the whole. For the physiocrats looked upon their proposed reforms, not as a result of temporary economic necessity, but as a rigid deduction from certain unassailable and immutable principles, newly discovered by their master Quesnay. At the basis was the conception of a self-perpetuating system of production and consumption whose pivot was agriculture. Cantillon had a few years earlier taken a similar view. He had pictured the whole country as dependent upon the landowners

who by their mode of living determine the economic activities of the nation. Industries are responsive to, and dependent upon, their demands, their humours, fashions, and style of life. These regulate the uses to which the soil shall be put, and thus determine indirectly the number of the inhabitants of the State."[1]

The same picture had presented itself to the eyes of Quesnay, who, however, reached more extreme conclusions. Rejecting the qualifications which Cantillon had introduced (such as the fact that certain artisans and other persons subsisted by foreign trade and were not dependent therefore upon the agriculture of their own country), Quesnay admitted agriculture alone among the productive powers of the nation and proceeded to pattern the political institutions of the country upon a purely agricultural basis. Agriculture, it is true, had a position of paramount importance in eighteenth-century France, and the low point to which it had sunk as a consequence of a policy of trade restrictions and of the worst anomalies of taxation made its resurrection all the more necessary. Quesnay, as is well known, considered industry and commerce purely sterile forces. The physiocrats were driven to this conclusion by the belief that only agriculture afforded what they called a *produit net*, that is, a rent over and above the costs of production and the entrepreneur's profits. That they were wrong on this point does not matter here, because it is to the further and more important developments that we must look.

A well-ordered agricultural system was the only way to stimulate the creation of capital greatly needed for productive purposes. The nation was starved and on the decline because not enough new capital was forthcoming, owing in part to its diversion into unproductive channels, in part to its destruction by an absurd system of taxation. A reform of the taxation system was, therefore, essential. The physiocrats saw that taxes should not hit production costs, if an undesirable and pernicious shifting process were to be avoided. Taxes ought to be levied only against what they called the *produit net* but which might more properly have been called "that part of the national dividend which is the necessary remuneration of the political class."

Physiocrats, by saying that land alone was capable of creating a net product and that tax ought to be laid exclusively on the same net product, did themselves involuntarily a great wrong. Let us for a moment drop the "net product" theory and focus our attention on its characteristics. Then, net product appears simply to be the free income of the landowning class. The income is free or disposable, because the recipient does not receive it as a compensation of an economic service. The recipient of the free income can live without being obliged to work or to attend to

[1] Higgs, *The Physiocrats*, pp. 36–37.

economic occupations. His time is therefore free and can be devoted to public service. His income, not being the necessary remuneration of an absorbing occupation,
can be diverted in part to public purposes. Nor must we put too much stress on
the fact that the "free" income goes to the "landowning" class. Physiocrats lived
amid a society whose principal source of free income was land. Capitalists, manu-
facturers, and merchants were too busy with their occupations to have much time
left for public service. Capitalists and merchants themselves, when rising to af-
fluency, bought land as a first step to nobility, and wishing to qualify their sons to
charges in the Courts of Judicature, in the Army, or in other Public Departments.[2]

The final point in this essentially modern and sound system of
taxation was that the state could not appropriate to its own use
the entire "free" part of the national income. It is in the description of the tragic consequences which would follow such an abuse
of the state's authority, as we shall see in a moment, that the best
clue is to be found of the real purposes behind the elaborate physiocratic construction of a system of legal despotism.

These reforms in taxation, however, would not have been suffi-
cient to divert to agriculture the needed flow of capital unless they
were accompanied by a sweeping grant of economic freedom and
by a complete abolition of trade restrictions, farm servitudes, and
petty feudal privileges. The restoration of an unhampered circulation of goods, including the free export of agricultural products,
constituted the logical conclusion of a process aiming at the re-
construction of the economic order on a foundation, not artificial
and capricious, but natural and permanent. That the new economic order was to be in direct relation to natural law was a
strongly embedded belief of the physiocrats. Indeed, Dupont
would not even admit, with Say, that political economy was the
science of wealth; he insisted upon defining it as the science of
natural law applied to civilized society. Thus economic freedom
was based upon foundations which seemed far more secure than
mere expediency. The appeal was not to convenience, but to a new
economic order having its origin in the doctrine of Quesnay, which
the physiocratic school had identified with the principles of natural
law. The economic cycle, the supremacy of agriculture, the system
of taxation, and economic freedom were its component parts. Upon
the general recognition of the importance of the first factor and
the practical enforcement of the others depended the rebirth of
an impoverished nation, prey to grave social unrest.

[2] I am indebted for this interpretation of the physiocratic doctrine of taxation to
Luigi Einaudi, "The Physiocratic Theory of Taxation," *Economic Essays in Honour
of Gustav Cassel* (London, 1933), pp. 131-132.

CHAPTER III

THE PHYSIOCRATIC SOURCES OF THE DOCTRINE
OF JUDICIAL CONTROL

BEFORE we proceed with the discussion of the main problem confronting us, it would appear advisable to describe briefly those writings by members of the physiocratic school which have constituted the primary sources of our study. Their number and variety will be apparent, as well as the high proportion of members of the school to whom may be attributed writings dealing with the doctrine of judicial review.

Even though François Quesnay's name is not commonly referred to in connection with the doctrine of judicial control, which he even seemed to ignore, any description of the literature on the subject must begin with him. He was the founder of the physiocratic school and exercised a great influence upon his followers, in whose works so much can properly be traced to the teachings of the old doctor. Even if he did not choose openly to discuss the issue, the following essays and notes by Quesnay yield some of the elements which later went into the formation of the school's doctrine of judicial control:

1. "Le Droit naturel," first published in the *Journal de l'agriculture, du commerce et des finances* (Paris, September 1765). The *Journal* had just then passed under physiocratic control (cf. Weulersse, *Le Mouvement physiocratique*, I, 95). Reprinted in *Oeuvres économiques et philosophiques de François Quesnay*, edited by Auguste Oncken (Frankfort et Paris, 1888), pp. 359–383. We shall refer to Oncken's standard edition.

2. "Despotisme de la Chine," first published in the *Ephémérides du citoyen* (Paris, March–June 1767). Reprinted in Oncken (pp. 563–660), who calls it a forerunner of Le Mercier's *L'Ordre naturel et essentiel des sociétés politiques*.

3. Notes to the unpublished "Traité de la Monarchie" by Mirabeau. Quesnay's notes are to be found in Weulersse, *Les Manuscripts économiques de François Quesnay et du Marquis de Mirabeau aux Archives Nationales* (Paris, 1910), pp. 20–29.

4. Notes to "Bref état des moyens pour la restauration de l'autorité du Roi et de ses finances," by Mirabeau. Both Mirabeau's essay and Quesnay's notes have been edited by Weulersse, *Revue d'histoire économique et sociale*, VI (1913), 177–211.

5. "Nécrologue de M. Quesnay de Saint-Germain, petit-fils du docteur Quesnay," par Dupont de Nemours, *Revue philosophique, littéraire et politique* (Paris, an XIII). Reprinted in Oncken, pp. 801–808. It contains a series of *Maximes*, ascribed by Dupont to Quesnay.

Mirabeau's name stands high among the physiocrats. Even without going to the length of declaring him to be the real founder of the school, it is true that the enthusiasm for the new doctrine which had descended upon him as if in heavenly revelation, the apostolic energy which he put into propagating it, his eminent position in the French nobility — all were powerful factors in the success which Quesnay's dogmas met in the sixties. Mirabeau alone had the privilege of being spared the brilliant sarcasm and the ridicule which Galiani poured upon the physiocratic school with the publication in 1769 of his *Dialogues sur le commerce des blés.* When the Abbé Le Gros undertook in 1787 the dissection of the physiocratic system [1] he based it on three works, two of which were Mirabeau's *Les Devoirs* (1780) and *Les Entretiens d'un jeune prince avec son gouverneur* (1785).

Mirabeau's significance cannot be lightly treated, and his writings cannot be dismissed simply because of their cumbersome, repetitious style, the vagueness of many of his assertions, and the obscurity of many of his pages. Furthermore, a distinction must be drawn between his earlier works, up to about 1769, and his later ones. The former are far superior; in them we shall find all of Mirabeau that need detain us here.

6. *Théorie de l'impôt* (Paris, 1760).
7. "La Dépravation, restauration et stabilité de l'ordre légal," a series of 18 letters published in the *Ephémérides du citoyen*, 1767–69.

The significance of Le Mercier's work for our purposes is greater than that of any other writer of the physiocratic school because he codified the doctrines which by 1767 were gaining currency as "physiocratiques" (the name given them by the Abbé Baudeau) and gave to a world striving for clarity and for coherent and nicely constructed systems of thought his *Ordre naturel et essentiel des sociétés politiques.* In forty-four chapters every aspect of the political, social, and economic doctrine of the school was made clear by the irresistible "force de l'évidence." By 1767 the school had succeeded in having in the *Ephémérides du citoyen* a periodical through which to carry on its propaganda work, and in *L'Ordre naturel* a text which could be relied upon to solve any possible difficulty. But Le Mercier's activity continued far beyond the golden

[1] *Analyse et examen du système des philosophes économistes par un solitaire* (Genève, Paris, 1787).

age of physiocracy, and a number of important works have to be recorded in his name, all marked by a notable unity of purpose.

8. *L'Ordre naturel et essentiel des sociétés politiques* (Paris, 1767), Depitre's edition (Paris, 1910). Daire, who edited in 1846 for the Guillaumin collection the most important works of the physiocratic school, thought that the first twenty-six chapters of Le Mercier's *L'Ordre* were "only a very confusing assemblage of precepts having to do at the same time with the moral order, politics, and the economic interests of society" (*Physiocrates*, 2nd part, p. 436), and entirely omitted them.

9. *L'Intérêt général de l'État, ou la liberté du commerce des blés, démontrée conforme au droit naturel; au droit public de la France; aux loix fondamentales du Royaume; à l'intérêt commun du Souverain et de ses sujets dans tous les temps* (Amsterdam, Paris, 1770).

10. *Lettre sur les économistes* (Paris, 1772).

11. "Mémoire sur l'instruction publique," in the September and October 1775 issue of the *Nouvelles Éphémérides économiques*, which the Abbé Baudeau published from December 1774 until June 1776.

12. *Les Voeux d'un Français, ou considérations sur les principaux objets dont le Roi et la Nation vont s'occuper* (Paris, 1788). This is the first of the new series of writings in which, as we shall later develop in detail, Le Mercier shifts his reasoning from philosophical to constitutional grounds.

13. *Essais sur les maximes et loix fondamentales de la Monarchie Française, ou Canevas d'un code constitutionnel* (Paris, 1789).

14. *L'Heureuse Nation, ou relation du gouvernement des féliciens, peuple souverainement libre sous l'empire absolu des loix* (Paris, 1792), 2 volumes.

A claim for coherence and for continued adherence to the doctrine of judicial control cannot be advanced by Dupont de Nemours. The revolution made him waver in the support he had given in his youth to the judicial guarantee as a means toward the achievement of the new political and economic order of physiocracy. He still clung to that ideal. But its fulfillment and permanence were to be secured through other avenues.

Le Mercier's work is the starting point for Dupont. When, at the end of 1767, a young man who had been shortly before admitted into Quesnay's circle, Dupont wrote his brief essay, *De l'origine et des progrès d'une science nouvelle*, he was entirely under the influence of the author of *L'Ordre naturel et essentiel des sociétés politiques*. The avowed purpose of the pamphlet was to summarize and make clear to a larger number of people the significance of Le Mercier's work, which, more often than not, lay hidden under a difficult language. The task was ably performed, and *De l'origine* remains the clearest general statement of the physiocratic doctrine. The same gift for clarity, if not for consistency, is to be found in the numerous subsequent writings which marked the long and active life of Dupont.

15. *De l'origine et des progrès d'une science nouvelle* (Paris, 1768, but written in 1767). Dubois edition (Paris, 1910).

16. *Physiocratie, ou constitution naturelle du gouvernement le plus avantageux au genre humain.* Recueil publié par Dupont (Leyde et Paris, 1768 [but 1767], 2 volumes). The first volume contains the introductory essay (101 pages) by Dupont. The rest is a collection of Quesnay's papers.

17. *Carl Friedrichs von Baden brieflicher Verkehr mit Mirabeau und Du Pont,* edited by Carl Knies (Heidelberg, 1892), 2 volumes. The letters cover the period from 1771 to 1806.

18. *Examen du gouvernement d'Angleterre comparé aux constitutions des Etats-Unis. Où l'on réfute quelques assertions contenues dans l'ouvrage de M. Adams, intitulé: Apologie des Constitutions des Etats-Unis d'Amérique, et dans celui de M. Delolme, intitulé: De la Constitution d'Angleterre. Par un cultivateur de New Jersey. Ouvrage traduit de l'anglois et accompagné de notes* (Paris, 1789). For a discussion of the authorship of this work, now definitely attributed to John Stevens, see below, p. 81. The notes are mostly by Dupont. They are among the most significant products of his pen, as they mark the abandonment of the attitude which he had taken, with regard to judicial control, in the earlier writings.

19. *De la périodicité des Assemblées Nationales, de leur organisation, de la forme à suivre pour amener les propositions qui pourront y être faites, à devenir des loix; et de la sanction nécessaire pour que ces loix soient obligatoires* (Paris, 1789).

20. *Projet d'articles relatifs à la constitution de l'Assemblée Nationale, à la forme de son travail, à la proposition, à la préparation, et à la sanction des loix.* Remis sur le Bureau de l'Assemblée Nationale, dans la séance de vendredi 4 septembre (1789).

21. *Constitution pour la République française. Du pouvoir législatif et du pouvoir exécutif convenables à la République française* (Paris, 1795).

22. *Observations sur la Constitution proposée par la Commission des onze, et sur la position actuelle de la France* (Paris, 1795).

23. *Philosophie de l'Univers* (Paris, 1796). But written in 1793, when Dupont was in hiding during the Terror.

24. *The Correspondence of Jefferson and Du Pont de Nemours,* edited by Gilbert Chinard (Baltimore, 1931). The letters cover the period from 1800 to 1816.

25. *Ephémérides du citoyen.* Founded by Baudeau in November 1765, this journal became, beginning January 1767, the organ of the physiocratic school. Its editorship was taken over by Dupont in May 1768, who gave it a new brilliancy and reputation. Dupont continued to direct the *Ephémérides* until its suppression in September 1772, upon the appearance of the third issue of that year.

We must now embrace in our survey less-known names. In 1768, when the newly born physiocratic school was struggling hard to win the favor of the King's entourage, no additions were more welcome than those of the sons of the great noble families. With particular rejoicing, then, did the school admit to its ranks the young Duke Paul François de la Vauguyon, son of the governor of the Dauphin. For during the next year, when the school definitely sought royal protection for its official organ, the *Ephémérides du citoyen,* the young Duke de la Vauguyon proved to be of the greatest value. An official dedication to the Dauphin had been nearly accepted when the entire arrangement fell through, very likely because of Mirabeau's strong opposition to any too great dependence upon the royal house.

But this is not La Vauguyon's contribution to the cause which interests us. When Le Mercier's *Ordre* drew a damaging retort from Mably, La Vauguyon was asked to answer the assertions of his very dangerous opponent. He did so in a series of five brilliant articles which appeared in the *Ephémérides*.

26. "Lettres de M. D. à M. l'Abbé de Mably," *Ephémérides du citoyen* (March to July 1768). Later in the year, when the articles were pieced together and published as a volume under the title *Doutes éclaircis*, Dupont wrote: "Cet ouvrage d'un homme de 22 ans . . . mérite de conserver une place distinguée parmi les livres classiques de la science la plus importante au genre humain," *Ephémérides* (1768), VII, 26. Barbier in his *Dictionnaire des ouvrages anonymes*, says that the volume was printed in a very limited number of copies. It was impossible to find one in the Bibliothèque Nationale. In the *Ephémérides* the five articles run to a total of well above 200 pages.

The subsequent career of La Vauguyon drew him apart from the school, which lost thereby the pen of a valuable polemist. He entered the army, succeeding his father in 1772 as peer of France. The new king appointed him minister to Holland in 1776 and ambassador to Spain in 1784. For five days, from the eleventh to the sixteenth of July 1789, he was Minister of Foreign Affairs. He resigned as a consequence of disagreement with the king following the fall of the Bastille. Jailed when he was on the point of leaving France, he was sent back to Madrid to be finally relieved of his duties in June 1790. At the end of 1795 we find him in Verona as one of the four ministers then forming Louis XVIII's council of state. But his too tolerant view of the revolutionists brought about his disgrace. In 1805 he went back to France and in 1814 was made a member of the House of Peers. For many years following his contribution to the physiocratic cause he was completely absorbed by his diplomatic career. Then came the revolution. It was only in 1816 that he took up the pen again, writing a *Tableau de la constitution française*. To him also belongs *De la simplification des principes constitutifs et administratifs, ou commentaire nouveau sur la charte constitutionnelle* (Paris, 1820). He died on March 14, 1828.[2]

[2] Biographical notes about La Vauguyon are found in the *Nouvelle biographie générale*; in Joseph-Marie Quérard, *La France littéraire* (Paris, 1827–64); and in Joseph Lardier, *Histoire biographique de la chambre des Pairs* (Paris, 1829).

Charles de Butré very likely considered the fifty thousand fruit trees which he had planted during his long life an achievement of greater importance than his writings on political and economic matters. Yet the latter offer some interesting sidelights and help prove the wide acceptance of the doctrine of judicial review among the followers of Quesnay. Baron Charles de Butré, born in Poitou in 1724, was a passionate agronomist all his life. As an equerry at the Court of Versailles he came in touch with Quesnay, under whose influence he fell. His connection with the physiocratic school dates back therefore to the earliest period. By 1763 he had left Versailles and retired to the country. In 1775 he succeeded Dupont as the adviser and friend of the margrave of Baden. For many years he resided at Karlsruhe, working as economic counselor first, as superintendent of forests and parks later. Caught by the Terror in Paris, his whole life was disrupted. Going to Strasbourg in 1797, he lived miserably on a small pension granted to him by the margrave. He died unnoticed in 1805.[3] His contributions to the doctrine of judicial review are to be found in the two following works:

27. "Lettre de M. K. à M. le Chevalier de **. Au sujet des doutes de M. l'abbé de Mably," *Ephémérides du citoyen* (1768), VI, 128–165. In an introductory note Dupont explains: "Cet auteur nous a demandé d'être désigné par la lettre K qui est la première de son nom dans une langue étrangère" (p. 122). There is little doubt of Butré's authorship. Teyssendier de la Serve confirms this (cf. *Mably et les Physiocrates*, Paris, 1911, p. 43). He adds, however, that a possible alternative might be the name of Carl Friedrich of Baden. This is scarcely possible since we know that the first *prise de contact* between the margrave and the physiocrats was through a letter which he addressed to Mirabeau on September 22, 1769 (cf. his correspondence edited by Knies, I, 3), and that his only contribution to the *Ephémérides* was the *Abrégé de l'économie politique*, published in 1772. Also, Butré's collaboration on the *Ephémérides* is confirmed by Reuss, *Charles de Butré*, p. 15. It was not, however, as Reuss states, very assiduous.

28. *Loix naturelles de l'agriculture et de l'ordre social* (Neuchâtel, 1781).

Like Butré, Le Trosne may be said to be nearer to Quesnay than to Le Mercier. Even if he did not tackle the problem of judicial control with the detail of other members of the physiocratic school, it cannot be doubted that he had accepted its principles. Furthermore, he brought to the discussion of the problems of government

---

[3] On Butré, cf. the monograph by Rodolphe Reuss, *Charles de Butré. Un physiocrate Tourangeau en Alsace et dans le Margraviat de Bade* (Paris, 1887). Some of Butré's letters to Carl Friedrich are to be found in the correspondence edited by Knies (see under no. 17), I, 113 ff.

and of the essence of constitutional rule a breadth of vision and a forcefulness of expression which entitle him to one of the foremost places among the followers of Quesnay.

29. *Discours sur l'état actuel de la magistrature et sur les causes de sa décadence.* Prononcé à l'ouverture des audiences du Bailliage d' Orléans, le 15 novembre, 1763 (Paris, 1764).

30. *De l'ordre social* (Paris, 1777).

31. *De l'intérêt social* (Paris, 1777). In the same volume with no. 30.

32. *De l'administration provinciale et de la réforme de l'impôt* (Basle, 1779), 2 volumes.

CHAPTER IV

THE PHYSIOCRATIC CONCEPT OF NATURAL ORDER

THE starting point of the physiocrats was the affirmation of the existence of a natural order based on rules which, if obeyed, would bring happiness to men, but which, if disregarded, would plunge them into disaster and misery. As Laski very aptly puts it:

> Their concern was to separate this scheme from the entanglements through which it had been concealed by the artificial contrivances of men. If, they thought, government could be so organised as to put the force of law behind the principles of this scheme, the happiness of men would be assured. For obedience to these principles, whether in government or in subjects, was necessary to right living. It was obedience to the law of man's nature given to him by the character of the universe in which he was involved. They did not doubt that these principles were as eternal and imprescriptible as those of physics. They conceived themselves, indeed, as doing for matters of social constitution what the great scientists of the seventeenth century had done for the physical universe. They were offering to statesmen a code of conduct which they evaded at their peril.[1]

Their system of natural order was removed from the metaphysical abstraction of the systems of natural law prevailing in the two preceding centuries. Theirs was not an ideal set of rules to be conceived as running parallel with the system of positive laws. Rather, they were anxious to hammer into men's minds the inevitable relationship which was to exist between the natural order and positive government. Once the existence of the order was admitted and its functioning made clear, it was idle to pretend that man could get along on something less than complete acceptance of its principles. The advocates of natural law could tolerate a lower, less perfect positive law, contenting themselves with casting a longing eye into the future in the hope of realizing a better world. The disciples of Quesnay could hardly assume such a detached attitude, because it was for them a question of life or death. Dupont writes on this point:

> Il y a un ordre naturel, essentiel et général, qui renferme les loix constitutives et fondamentales de toutes les sociétés; un ordre duquel les sociétés ne peuvent s'écarter sans être moins sociétés, sans que l'état politique ait moins de consistance, sans que ses membres se trouvent plus ou moins désunis et dans une situation violente; un

[1] Harold Laski, *The Rise of Liberalism* (London and New York, 1936), pp. 207–208.

ordre qu'on ne pourrait abandonner entièrement sans opérer la dissolution de la société et bientôt la destruction absolue de l'espèce humaine.[2]

This changed attitude towards natural law is made clear by Quesnay in his discussion of natural rights. Natural rights, he says, cannot be enjoyed unless there exists a positive order behind them. Writing in a vein which was then not very common in France, Quesnay stresses the fact that only in organized society can natural rights yield those fruits which are otherwise vainly expected of them:

La jouissance de leur droit naturel doit être fort bornée dans cet état de pure nature et d'indépendance, où nous ne supposons encore entr'eux aucun concours pour s'entr'aider mutuellement, et où les forts peuvent user injustement de violence contre les faibles. Lorsqu'ils entreront en société et qu'ils feront entre eux des conventions pour leur avantage réciproque, ils augmenteront donc la jouissance de leur droit naturel, et ils s'assureront même la pleine étendue de cette jouissance, si la constitution de la société est conforme à l'ordre évidemment le plus avantageux aux hommes relativement aux lois fondamentales de leur droit naturel.[3]

He might have added that civil society is so far from being an instrument for the realization of abstract rights, that the individual, whatever his metaphysical rights, only through his active belonging to society can acquire rights — real, definite, and worth possessing. The abstract perfection of a right spells its practical doom, since the more a right escapes rationally the limitations imposed by practical circumstances, the greater are the restrictions it must encounter when its application to a given social system is first attempted.

Any explicit statement to that effect was too much perhaps to expect from a French writer of the middle of the eighteenth century, even though he did imply substantial acceptance of the principle. And we must not be surprised, therefore, at the language used by the most typically rationalist and French member of the school, Le Mercier de la Rivière. Every word of his bears the imprint of his period's rationalism. He seems to imply, in at least a part of his reasoning, the existence of two parallel sets of rules, the natural and the positive orders. Society has to rely on two types of laws, the natural and the positive. The former are essential and common to all men. Their necessity is manifest, even though they do not find expression in any outward sign, and even though they are not included in any ordinary collection of laws. They are to be

[2] Dupont, *De l'origine*, p. 7.
[3] "Droit naturel," *Oeuvres*, p. 368.

found in the code of nature, and it is there, helped by our rational faculties, that we can read them. The test of the validity of positive law, which rules man's everyday actions, is in its compatibility and inner concordance with the standard of natural law. It is in the spirit then of the law, not in its letter, that is to be found "le premier principe d'une soumission constante." [4]

But for Le Mercier, too, the principle of interdependence between natural order and positive law reasserts itself. When the connection is broken, when men refuse to accept the inevitable consequences of the rules established by natural order, then the state of equilibrium which keeps society going is broken, and men are cast forth into the wilderness.

It is here that the physiocrats differentiate themselves from other schools of natural law. When Leibnitz wants to translate his ideals into concrete terms he will advocate a *Werkhaus* or a *Kaufhaus*, that is, institutions which imply the right of members of society to work and to the fruits of their work. When the physiocrats are talking of their natural order they have in mind something different.

Their "order" is a given set of principles upon the rejection or acceptance of which will depend the fate of civil society. If private property is respected; if men are left free to buy and to sell, to initiate trade and industry, to export or import goods; if taxes are levied upon those able to shoulder the burden, then society will prosper and grow. Otherwise it will decay and disappear as a civilized community.

The physiocratic ideal lies in a conformity between the positive laws issued by the prince and that "order" which they have discovered as *optimum bonum*. To force the prince to comply with the order's rules, most of the members of the school are anxious to set up a supreme magistracy with the task of declaring void those legislative acts which are issued in defiance to the order. But should the magistrates fail to declare those acts void or should the prince fail at all to enact the order, the physiocrats would not believe their "order" to be alive. It would not even have that peculiar life which belongs to the "natural social law," as expounded by the distinguished Russian legal philosopher, George Gurvitch.[5]

---

[4] Le Mercier, *L'Ordre naturel*, p. 58.
[5] *L'Idée du droit social* (Paris, 1931). Cf. especially the second part, "L'École du 'droit social naturel' et les physiocrates," pp. 171 ff.

The physiocrats do not say that there is a juridical conflict between state and society and that in this conflict society prevails over the state.[6] They say that, whenever the positive laws issued by the prince are in contradiction of the "order," these consequences will inevitably follow: (a) agriculture will decay; (b) merchants and financiers will grow rich; (c) wealth will leave the kingdom; (d) workers will become poor, and unemployment will spread; (e) the majority will little by little be reduced to a condition of servitude towards the state; (f) first society and then the state will get weaker and will decay; (g) a foreign enemy will seize and destroy the state.

Of all physiocratic writers none described this process with clearer vision than Mirabeau. He was anxious to distinguish himself from Montesquieu, whose guides had been "le génie et l'érudition." His guide was going to be "l'ordre naturel."

Beyond the variety of positive laws Mirabeau is in search of a "fondement assuré, immuable, indépendant des passions humaines et des circonstances particulières." [7] He found this immutable foundation of political speculation as early as 1760, when in the *Théorie de l'impôt* he showed the inevitable connection between tyranny and social decay. Tyranny was present when the sovereign appropriated to his personal use the whole of the "free" part of national income. Then the sovereign, instead of being the interpreter of the order, "would become the fountain of all power and favor, thereby conducing human society to a decadent state." [8] Every existing bulwark between organized society and anarchy would be slowly destroyed in a state where the sovereign had become omnipotent and supreme master of the economic lives of his subjects, in a state which had not been careful to circumscribe the sovereign power on all sides by a system of guarantees. Mirabeau's words deserve quotation in full:

Si le Prince, dit-on, enlevoit par un impôt exorbitant tous les revenus, quel mal en arriveroit-il? Les revenus ne rentreroient-ils pas annuellement par ses dépenses dans la circulation, et ne feroient-ils pas vivre de la sorte toutes les classes d'usufruitiers, de gagistes, d'artisans, et de travailleurs de tout genre?

Il en arriveroit, 1° Qu'il n'y auroit plus qu'un centre de distribution, et qu'une ville dans le Royaume.

2° Qu'on ne seroit occupé qu'à obtenir des places et des emplois à la cour,

---

[6] Gurvitch, *L'Idée du droit social*, p. 249.

[7] "Restauration de l'ordre légal" (fourth letter), *Ephémérides du citoyen* (1768), VI, 11, 13.

[8] Luigi Einaudi, in *Economic Essays*, p. 134.

qu'à solliciter des augmentations de gages et des pensions, qu'à participer aux libéralités du Prince, qu'à éviter le travail, qu'à parvenir à la fortune par toutes les voyes de collusion que la cupidité peut suggérer, qu'à multiplier les abus dans l'ordre de la distribution et des dépenses.

3° Comme l'homme quelconque n'est qu'un, et ne sçauroit régir avec indépendance que ce qu'il voit et touche, le propriétaire universel seroit dépendant pour toute la portion de sa propriété qui seroit hors de sa portée. Le Gouvernement des biens seroit donc livré à l'Agence, c'est-à-dire, à des particuliers à qui la propriété seroit étrangere et qui ne penseroient qu'à leur propre fortune, et à celles de leurs coopérateurs dans l'oeuvre d'iniquité.

4° Tout agent qui songe à son propre fait, est forcé à conniver aux déprédations des autres, d'où s'ensuit que tout à la Cour dégéneroit en brigandage.

5° Que ceux que le Souverain enrichiroit, précipiteroient les dépenses du côté du luxe de décoration et de fantaisie, attendu que le bon usage des richesses mal acquises est un phénomene ici bas, attendu encore que pour sentir le prix de la richesse, il faut l'avoir péniblement acquise.

6° Le petit nombre même d'entre ces privilégiés, qui voudroient acquerir des biens et assurer des revenus à leur postérité, porteroient leurs richesses chez l'étranger, sçachant bien que rien n'est assuré dans le pays, ou chercheroient à se faire des fonds sur l'Etat, fonds d'une nature sourde et fragile, mais rongeurs des gains et des facultés d'autrui, et par là même, ressorts actifs de la révolution.

7° La culture livrée à des manoeuvres précaires, et par tant de voies accumulées privée de richesses, ne feroit que languir, les revenus diminueroient chaque jour, et s'anéantiroient enfin.

8° Les Courtisans et les Favoris profiteroient de l'enfance et de la caducité des Souverains pour s'emparer des revenus du fisc, et pour acquerir une puissanse dangereuse à l'Etat et au Souverain.

9° La noblesse, sans patrie et sans possessions, seroit réduite à un service militaire purement mercénaire, tandis que la solde équitable et l'entretien nécessaire seroient refusés au soldat.

10° La magistrature, n'ayant plus de propriétés, la Justice seroit vénale, et les loix mêmes seroient un mal; car il ne faut plus de loix, où il n'y a plus de propriété, et le vain simulacre de celles qui demeureroient encore, ne seroit plus qu'un spectre favorable à l'injustice: je le répete, il ne faudroit plus de loix, et sans loix, que devient la société et l'Etat?

11° Il n'y auroit que les commerçans qui, indépendamment d'une constitution d'Etat si désunie, si bouleversée et si passagere, pourroient assembler des richesses, et se former, par leurs correspondances avec les autres nations, des possessions ou des propriétés assurées. De là naîtroit dans la Nation, un Etat républicain et nécessaire, qui éluderoit la domination absurde et désordonnée.

12° L'oppression enfin ayant appris au peuple le secret de Diogène, de jeter sa tasse et de boire dans le creux de sa main, il s'abandonneroit à la paresse et à une orgueilleuse indigence, et vivroit dans l'oisiveté et dans l'indépendance. Le tableau de l'Etat et de la société ne conserveroit plus que le cadre facile à rompre par le moindre effort étranger. . . . En un mot, un Etat où le tribut enleveroit le revenu du territoire, seroit un Etat en pleine anarchie, sans consistance et sans durée.[9]

The only hope of salvation lies in the adoption of the principles of the physiocratic "order": "Voilà donc une législation toute faite, toute naturelle, divine, universelle, immuable, à laquelle les

[9] Mirabeau, *Théorie de l'impôt*, pp. 167–171.

hommes ne peuvent rien ajouter que du désordre." [10] Men cannot legislate at will, their freedom to do so is everywhere subordinated to the rule of natural order, "qui seule a vraiment droit de nous donner des lois." [11]

The true claim to fame of the physiocrats is their creation of economic science. This claim is justified because:

(1) They substituted for fragmentary and disjointed observation of economic problems a unitary, comprehensive, and well-rounded analysis, such as is not to be found even in Adam Smith. They grasped, by virtue of Quesnay's *Tableau*, and despite its obscurity, the conception of the ever moving cycle of production.

(2) They substituted for the traditional suggestions of new legislative enactments to remedy existing economic ills the study of cause and effect. The reasoning is as follows:

(a) The observation of facts, coupled with historical experience, shows the existence of a natural order which, if followed, allows human societies to prosper.

(b) The same observation shows the existence of positive laws and institutions which prevent the realization of that order: ill-conceived systems of taxation, shackles to the free movements of commerce, monopolies, and privileges — all productive of losses and attrition.

(c) If the prince, helped by his counselors and supervised by the magistrates, repeals the bad laws and in their place declares other laws which are in harmony with the "natural and essential order of human societies," there will follow the prosperity of both the state and its citizens.

(d) If the prince embarks upon a different policy, there will follow the decay and the ultimate ruin of both the state and its citizens.

The physiocrats therefore do not call forth a contrast between state and society; they inquire into the reasons which cause the flourishing or the decadence of both at the same time. The celebrated words of Dupont are the most fitting summary that can be given of the physiocratic doctrine: "Impositions indirectes;

[10] "Dépravation de l'ordre légal" (first letter), *Ephémérides du citoyen* (1767), IX, 86.

[11] "Restauration de l'ordre légal" (second letter), *Ephémérides du citoyen* (1768), IV, 74.

pauvres paysans. Pauvres paysans; pauvre royaume. Pauvre royaume; pauvre souverain." [12]

Here Dupont is indicating a logical sequence, in which the violation of the natural order is indicated by the imposition of indirect taxes. He may have been right or wrong in thus concentrating upon that single point. But this is not important. What matters is that the physiocrats did not waste their energies in contrasting an ideal system of natural law with the existing system of positive law. They undertook to discover the causes which favor or hamper social progress.

It was the physiocrats' belief that in the long run the physiocratic order would inevitably assert itself even upon an unwilling world. In the struggle between countries, that country would win which acted in conformity with the order. But this would have been a lengthy, costly, ruinous process. Was it not better, now that science had discovered the key to human prosperity and happiness, to go about the business of improving existing maladjustments at once?

In the end the physiocrats, too, suggest remedies to the prince; they, too, become legislators, with a burning desire to see the king of France translate into reality the principles of the natural order. These are, however, but practical applications and do not constitute the core of their doctrine. Their true contribution, as we have said, is to be found in their insistence that societies and states are ruled by laws and that given certain premises α certain consequences a will follow; whereas, given certain premises β, other consequences b will follow. Therefore, whoever wants to attain a must be ruled by α and not by β; and whoever wants to attain b must be ruled by β and not by α.[13]

[12] *De l'origine*, p. 23.

[13] The best analysis of the real significance of physiocratic economic thought is to be found in Joseph Schumpeter, *Epochen der Dogmen- und Methodengeschichte*, Grundriss der Sozialökonomik (Tübingen, 1914), I, 39–50.

CHAPTER V

THE MEANS FOR THE REALIZATION OF THE NATURAL ORDER OF PHYSIOCRACY

1. LEGAL DESPOTISM

WHAT were, under the existing political circumstances, the means to be used for the success of the physiocratic "order?" What power was strong enough to guarantee that property, liberty, and security which Quesnay and his followers considered as the foundations of the state? That "tutelary authority" was found by the physiocrats in the royal power. The reasons which prompted the physiocrats to look in that direction have never been better analyzed than by Tocqueville, whose words cannot be improved upon:

Political liberty had been destroyed for so long in France, that its conditions and effects had been almost completely forgotten. One can even add that political liberty had been rendered suspect and was often looked upon with prejudice by reason of the nameless remnants of it which had survived and of the institutions which seemed to have been created to supplant it. Most of the "assemblées d'états" which still existed had retained, with outdated procedure, a mediaeval spirit and hampered rather than aided the progress of society; Parliaments, functioning alone as political bodies, could not prevent the bad, and often prevented the good, governmental actions.

To accomplish the revolution which was in their thoughts with the help of these old institutions seemed impossible [to the physiocrats]; equally disliked by them was the idea of entrusting the execution of their plans to a self-governing nation: how, indeed, could one have an entire nation adopt and follow a system of reforms so complex and so closely interrelated? The easiest and wisest thing to do was to make the royal administration subservient to their plans.

This new power has not emerged from mediaeval institutions; of them it carries no trace; for all its errors, certain good tendencies are to be detected. It shares with them a natural inclination for equality of conditions and uniformity of rules; with them it hates, secretly, all the old institutions born of feudalism and tending toward aristocracy. One would vainly search the rest of Europe for a machine of government equally well organized, equally great and powerful. To find such a government at home seems to them a particularly happy circumstance.[1]

After such a sagacious analysis it is to be regretted that Tocqueville failed to see the true nature of the despotism which the physi-

---

[1] Tocqueville, *Ancien régime*, pp. 260–261. A similar interpretation is to be found in, among others, Lavergne, *Economistes français du XVIIIe siècle*, p. 31; Petzet, *Der Physiokratismus*, pp. 117–119. Schelle (*Du Pont*, pp. 94–96), losing sight of the larger issue, does not seem to accept this view and laments the fact that the political doctrines of the physiocrats had been concocted by them merely in an effort to flatter the princes.

ocrats wished to set up. It is clear that their monarch was a limited one, a legal despot, as they unhappily chose to call him, existing only for certain well-defined purposes and no others. The sovereign or tutelary authority did not exist to make laws, for the laws were already all there, the work of divine will and expressing the fundamental principles of the natural order. The only duty of the sovereign in a physiocratic state was to interpret these natural laws and to apply them with the help of positive laws to particular cases and to the conduct of the everyday affairs of the kingdom.

The despot was but a means towards the achieving of an end. That this is so is proved beyond doubt by the constant fear which is present in all physiocratic writings lest the despot should go beyond the limits assigned to him and, by violating the rules of the natural order, should set up an absolute, centralized power.

Mirabeau offers the best explanation of the system of guarantees and of the reasons which led the physiocrats to consider them essential in their doctrine of government.[2] In order that the process of decadence, which Mirabeau ascribes to a violation of the natural economic order, might be avoided, (a) the sovereign was obliged to spread far and wide the knowledge of the law on which the order was founded, so that citizens might better resist all encroachments upon it; and (b) a control of all positive laws was to be vested in the judiciary. Thus, above the despot was set the judicial guarantee.

The judicial guarantee was the crowning feature of a doctrine rooted in the necessity of bringing radical reform to France in order to save her from revolution. Given certain basic assumptions on which a system of government had been reared, the physiocrats were forced to the conclusion that in order to avoid subsequent nullification of that system, power was to be located somewhere to insure its permanence. That ultimate power, they said, was to reside in the highest judges of the land. From this premise a doctrine of judicial control was developed, which, as we shall see, went far beyond the traditional constitutional doctrine of France. For it cannot be denied that, notwithstanding the great powers of control granted to Parliament by the French constitutionalists of the two preceding centuries, the ultimate overruling power of the king had not been seriously challenged within Parliament itself.

[2] Cf. above, p. 23.

2. Judicial Control

The various members of the physiocratic school contributed to the discussion of the problem of control through the judiciary with writings of different import, but all marked by a singular unity of purpose. Following, roughly, the criterion of the increasing intensity with which our problem has been discussed, we shall begin with Quesnay and Mirabeau, examine Le Trosne, Butré, and La Vauguyon, and conclude with Le Mercier and Dupont.

Quesnay was to a great extent content with stressing the existence of the natural order. This may explain in part the lack of open reference to the issue of judicial review. His first approach to the problem of how to control the sovereign power, which to him, as to all other physiocrats in the best bodinian tradition was not limitless, was through the *états généraux*.

In some interesting marginal notes to a fragment on the nobility written by Mirabeau between 1758 and 1760 (and showing his usual attachment to the privileges of the nobility), Quesnay points out that a monarchy cannot very well survive with only a king and a cabinet: "C'est un corps, comme on le dit, qui change continuellement de tête; ainsi, abandonné à la tête, c'est le livrer à l'inconstance la plus dangereuse." What are needed are

des assemblées d'Etats; mais les monarques les évitent . . . Il faut pourtant ou de ces Assemblées, ou un Conseil aulique permanent et nombreux des prudes de toutes les classes, pour la direction générale du royaume. Sans quoi, il est inutile de parler monarchie; car autrement la monarchie ne peut être qu'une folle le glaive à la main.[3]

The idea of a limited council seems to him more feasible, and he discusses it again:

Il est essentiel que le Roi ait un conseil permanent composé de douze ou quinze personnes choisies dans la noblesse et dans la magistrature, afin de maintenir un plan fixe de gouvernement qui puisse se soutenir contre les abus et l'administration arbitraire de l'autorité confiée, et qui dans la minorité et dans la faiblesse de la vieillesse des souverains assure la solidité et l'immutabilité du gouvernement.[4]

But Quesnay is faced with a reality which proves that bad positive laws are frequent: "La multitude des lois contradictoires et absurdes établies successivement chez les nations, prouve manifeste-

[3] Weulersse, *Les Manuscrits de Quesnay et de Mirabeau*, p. 27.
[4] Quesnay's note to "Bref état des moyens pour la restauration de l'autorité du Roi et de ses finances, par le Marquis de Mirabeau," edited by Weulersse, in *Revue d'histoire économique et sociale*, VI (1913), 186–187.

ment que les lois positives sont sujettes à s'écarter souvent des règles immuables de la justice et de l'ordre naturel le plus avantageux à la société." [5] Mere external checks are not enough, and an appeal is thereupon made to the conscience of the legislators themselves: they should be the ones to repeal the unjust laws which they had passed without recourse to a firm rational basis: "Les lois humaines sont quelquefois surprises par des motifs dont la raison éclairée ne reconnait pas toujours la justice; ce qui oblige ensuite la sagesse des législateurs d'abroger des lois qu'ils ont faites eux-mêmes." [6] Only ignorance can favor the introduction of positive laws contrary to the rational and natural order. "Si le flambeau de la raison y éclaire le gouvernement, toutes les lois positives nuisibles à la société et au souverain, disparaîtront." [7]

The torch of reason, however, cannot illuminate the legislators if there is not the fire of natural law to put it aflame. Quesnay, the discoverer of the existence of those natural laws in the economic field which he had expounded in his *Tableau économique*, was not laggard in recognizing the existence and importance of natural laws in the political field, too. Indeed, he may be said to be the real originator of much of the physiocratic doctrine in this respect. While his coöperative work with Mirabeau in the economic sphere is well known, it is not always realized how much he contributed, for instance, to Le Mercier's *De l'ordre naturel et essentiel des sociétés politiques*. Quite apart from any actual editorial help given by Quesnay to Mercier,[8] it is clear that the publication, begun in March 1767 in the *Ephémérides du citoyen*, of Quesnay's essay "Despotisme de la Chine," was intended to set the pace for the school's speculations in the realm of the science of politics.

Natural laws cannot be interfered with by legislators, who have not contributed to their formation. The sovereign authority can and must establish laws to remedy any disorderly condition existing in the state, but it cannot "empiéter sur l'ordre naturel de la société." [9] Man is not "l'instituteur de ces lois qui fixent l'ordre des opérations de la nature"; the gardener can prune the tree, but

---

[5] "Droit naturel," *Oeuvres*, p. 366.

[6] *Ibid.*

[7] *Ibid.*, p. 376.

[8] "J'ai vu l'auteur de *l'Ordre naturel et essentiel des sociétés politiques* travailler six semaines entières en robe de chambre dans l'entresol du docteur [Quesnay], fondre et refondre son ouvrage." Letter of Mirabeau to Longo, May 27, 1788 (Louis Léonard de Loménie, *Les Mirabeau* [Paris, 1879], II, 334).

[9] "Despotisme de la Chine," *Oeuvres*, p. 642.

he cannot skin it: "La constitution de l'arbre est l'ordre naturel même, réglé par des lois essentielles et irréfragables, qui ne doivent point être dérangées par des lois étrangères." [10] In China, that happy country where natural law rules supreme, the constitution, which embodies the fundamental principles of natural law, is safeguarded by making it entirely independent from the emperor, who has no power to change it.[11] Should the emperor try to violate the constitution and enforce laws which are contrary to its spirit, then the whole judicial system of the country would be set in motion to oppose such an attempt. "Il n'y a peut-être pas de pays où l'on passe des remontrances au souverain avec plus de liberté qu'à la Chine." [12] These protests, in which, besides the tribunals, great state officials such as the mandarins join, are always successful, concludes Quesnay, because ferocious and recalcitrant emperors are very rare in China.

It is no wonder, then, that when Quesnay tried to translate the precepts which he had learned from his study of the Chinese constitution into maxims which should serve as a model for *all* countries,[13] his thought should go back to those Chinese magistrates, whose recognized duty was to uphold the constitution, and whose word of approval was necessary to give validity to the emperor's laws.[14] Quesnay's plea is that the jurisdiction of tribunals should not be narrowed down to the mere interpretation of positive laws; it should include consideration of the prime principles of natural law. This ought to be, since their duty is the "verification" of positive laws, that is, a determination of the compatibility of positive and natural laws, the latter embodied presumably in the constitution. Here are the actual words used by Quesnay in a passage which does not seem to have received the attention it deserves:

Les tribunaux qui seraient bornés à l'intelligence littérale des lois de la justice distributive, ne remonteraient pas aux principes primitifs du droit naturel, du droit public et du droit des gens. Il n'en est pas moins avantageux pour l'Etat que ces compagnies augustes, chargées de la vérification et du dépôt des lois positives, étendent leurs connaissances sur les lois naturelles, qui sont par essence les lois fondamentales de la société et les sources des lois positives.[15]

[10] *Ibid.*, pp. 642–643.
[11] *Ibid.*, p. 607.
[12] *Ibid.*, p. 608.
[13] *Ibid.*, chap. VIII.
[14] *Ibid.*, p. 606. Quesnay's high opinion of the judges is well illustrated by his definition of them: "le corps moral de la nation, c'est-à-dire la partie pensante du peuple" (quoted in Cheinisse, *Les Idées politiques*, p. 115).
[15] "Despotisme de la Chine," *Oeuvres*, p. 640.

What he actually meant by "vérification" Quesnay did not say. Nor did he stipulate how far the judges could go in their control of positive law. But, in the light of everything he said, the conclusions drawn by Dupont de Nemours some forty years later seem entirely valid. In summing up Quesnay's doctrine in a funeral eulogy of one of his grandsons, Dupont attributes this conception of *law* and *ordinance* to Quesnay.

Les lois sont irrévocables, elles tiennent à l'essence des hommes et des choses; elles sont l'expression de la volonté de Dieu; et plus on y réfléchit, plus on les révère. Les *ordonnances* sont l'ouvrage des hommes. Elles ont pour objet l'exécution des lois. La soumission provisoire leur est due pour le maintien de l'*ordre*. Mais il est dans leur nature de demeurer sujettes à l'examen, et d'être révocables quand il devient *évident* qu'elles ne sont pas d'accord avec les lois.[16]

It would seem that in these words we have the fundamental elements of that doctrine of judicial control which Quesnay's followers were to develop still further.

The position of Mirabeau is less clear. But from his early negative position of merely warning the sovereign of the existence of a natural order which had to be followed if certain destruction was to be avoided, we are able to detect a change in the years when the physiocratic school was in full bloom and the doctrine of judicial control had already received wide discussion. The change is real, even if rendered less perceptible by a thick veil of contradictions and obscure phrasing.

In the fifth issue of the *Ephémérides du citoyen* of 1769 Mirabeau published the eighteenth and final letter of his famous series on the degeneration, restoration, and stability of the legal order. It was a summary in which Mirabeau tried to make clear his position. He admits at once the existence of forces of disruption, of particularistic and exclusive interests, which inevitably will run counter to natural laws and try to make the government subservient to their ends. But such forces and such interests, such deviation of the government from its true path, must be fought:

Mais, là où il règne la connaissance de la *justice par essence*, où se montre l'évidence des lois naturelles, où l'une et l'autre se perpétuent par l'instruction, là l'opinion générale s'oppose aux erreurs de l'administration, là l'administration elle-même se refuse à servir les erreurs du gouvernement.[17]

[16] "Nécrologue de M. Quesnay de St. Germain, par D. P. D. N.," *Oeuvres*, p. 803.
[17] *Ephémérides du citoyen* (1769), V, 9.

It is strange to see Mirabeau put so much confidence in the administration in his fight against oppressive governments, since the administrative bodies would, as a rule, be deprived of really efficient means of conducting the battle. He seemed to realize the shortcomings of his proposition almost as soon as he had finished putting on paper the words we have quoted. Had he really fully expressed his thoughts in his series of letters on the legal order, "on aurait vu *l'autorité législative* d'une part, *et le droit et le pouvoir négatif* de l'autre, fondé également sur la justice par essence." [18] It seems clear that in using the words *pouvoir négatif* as a sort of counterpart to the *autorité législative*, Mirabeau had in mind a body whose duty it would have been to check the activities of the legislative, with powers to deny its approval to measures passed in violation of the principles of "essential justice." Whether this body was to assume judicial nature it is difficult to tell. That the *pouvoir négatif* could be the judiciary seems altogether unlikely. Mirabeau never speaks of such power as belonging to the judges, and even in the eighteenth letter he defines their duty as follows: "La magistrature préposée par l'autorité à la dénonciation de la loi civile dans les cas particuliers; voilà l'application de la loi." [19] This seems to take away from the judges the cognizance of natural laws and leave them nothing more than the interpretation of civil law in the individual cases in dispute. What the passage quoted can be made to say is that, while in all earlier writings Mirabeau had been satisfied to leave to nature the redress of the ills deriving from a bad government, failure of which would lead inevitably to a period of decadence and the ultimate ruin of the state, he took a very different attitude in 1769 with the admission that a negative power was essential to balance the legislative power, which included in it, according to the physiocratic theory, the executive power also. Only one explanation can be given of the change which caused Mirabeau to accept the substance of what had by then become the established doctrine of the physiocratic school with regard to the necessity of limitations upon the sovereign power: he had fallen under the influence of Le Mercier de la Rivière's book published in 1767, *L'Ordre naturel et essentiel des sociétés politiques*. Although he failed to give the system of guarantees against

---

[18] *Ephémérides du citoyen* (1769), V, 11.
[19] *Ibid.*, V, 101.

the legal despot, particularly the judicial guarantee, the development given to it by Le Mercier, Mirabeau had accepted the essential principles underlying it. Thus, even though he did not dwell on the problem of judicial control in his later works, it is very likely that on this issue the coincidence of his views with those of the other members of the physiocratic school was greater than has been commonly assumed.

The same can be said of one less known but not less distinguished member of the school, the magistrate Le Trosne, who in his *De l'ordre social* gave to France, at a time when the physiocratic school had begun to fade in the background, the picture of what the social order it had advocated was like. He uses, far more than his predecessors, a juridical language; in him the greater emphasis on positive legislation takes away the stigma of an exaggerated rational abstraction. And he mellowed his individualism with a good deal of historical common sense. To him what mattered was the unbroken chain of generations following one another.[20] He also wanted, notwithstanding his apparent agreement with the school's traditional doctrine of legal despotism, a *conseil national*, restricted in numbers, but "vraiment le représentant de la nation." [21] Such a national council, elected through provincial assemblies and restricted in its duties only to the consideration of fiscal problems, was inevitably to assume those larger functions which Le Trosne's very words indicate.

Il faut que toute la Nation, qui semble aujourd'hui privée de vie et d'action, qui n'a qu'une sorte d'existence passive, devienne animée et organisée dans toutes ses parties, pour former un véritable corps social . . . Il est de l'essence de tout corps civil, de toute société, d'exister ou par la réunion de ses membres, ou, si elle est trop nombreuse, par celle de ses Représentants. Ôter à une nation le droit d'avoir des Représentants, c'est la dissoudre, c'est la réduire à n'être plus une société civile.[22]

Because of the eminent position taken by this body of representatives of the people, the issue of judicial control seems to fade in the background in Le Trosne's work. Le Trosne even appears content to assume Mirabeau's fatalistic view of the catastrophic

---

[20] *De l'ordre social* (Paris, 1777), p. 285.

[21] *De l'administration provinciale et de la réforme de l'impôt* (Basle, 1779), I, 568.

[22] *De l'administration provinciale*, I, 534, 540. For a discussion of Turgot's and Le Trosne's proposals of a national assembly, see A. Esmein, "L'Assemblée nationale proposée par les Physiocrates," *Séances et travaux de l'Académie des Sciences morales et politiques*, CLXII (Paris, 1904), 397 ff.

consequences that will befall every civil society which has forgotten to live by the rules of the "essential order." This is what has happened in the past.

L'autorité souveraine constituée pour maintenir l'observation des loix simples qui avoient présidé à la réunion, pour protéger la société au dehors, pour réprimer au dedans toute usurpation, toute violation des droits légitimes, a oublié le motif de son institution, et a passé les bornes de sa jurisdiction naturelle, au-delà desquelles il ne peut y avoir que désordre. Dès-lors les passions et les intérêts particuliers exclusifs ont commencé à gouverner tous les rapports, à porter le trouble dans le sein des sociétés, et à les diviser entre elles. Au dedans la puissance tutélaire qui n'a qu'un pouvoir d'exécution, a entrepris de dicter des loix: elle a contrarié par des ordres arbitraires, injustes, oppresseurs, cette législation divine, qu'il ne s'agissait que de reconnoître, d'observer et de faire observer, et a porté dans les relations intérieures de la société un désordre légal beaucoup plus difficile à réformer, que celui qui ne précède que de la violence.[23]

The future should differ from the past, according to Le Trosne, and the revelation of the new order should prevent the sovereign from forgetting the very reason of its institution. How to keep within certain boundaries the activity of the sovereign legislative power seems, therefore, to be the chief problem before the new government, and Le Trosne considers it as such. To say, as a commentator does, that Le Trosne leaves the interpretation and application of the rules of the order to the will of the king alone, "without ever thinking of restricting the king's powers or of controlling his administration" [24] (even with the qualification, it is true, that the sovereign's duties are small), overlooks the fact that the sovereign in Le Trosne's state is bound to follow strictly the path of constitutional laws, and that, more than any other physiocratic writer, Le Trosne is anxious to increase the value of public opinion as a check upon government.

There are three types of laws, according to Le Trosne. First come the unwritten fundamental laws, "les loix de la justice absolue et essentielle," then, the constitutional laws, which establish "l'autorité souveraine, son dépôt dans telle ou telle main, l'ordre de la

---

[23] Le Trosne, De l'ordre, pp. 59–60. This vivid and apt description of the violation of the laws of the international order follows: "L'amour de la patrie a pris un esprit exclusif qu'il ne doit point avoir. Chaque société s'est crue autorisée à regarder son intérêt comme contraire à celui des autres, et à circonscrire dans les bornes étroites de son territoire l'observation des devoirs que la justice impose. La qualité d'étranger a entraîné en quelque sorte l'idée d'ennemi. On n'a pas craint d'exercer au dehors les crimes et les violences qu'on jugeoit indispensable de réprimer au dedans: de menacer l'indépendance et la propriété de ses voisins, et d'employer à l'attaque la force publique uniquement destinée à la protection et à la défense" (De l'ordre, p. 60).

[24] Jérôme Mille, Un Physiocrate oublié, G. F. Le Trosne (Paris, 1905), p. 61.

succession, les droits et les fonctions des corps intermédiaires . . .
la formation des loix positives";[25] finally, the civil, or positive laws,
which take care of administrative details and of the varying needs
of the community.

Now Le Trosne sees in the permanence of and the respect for
the constitutional laws the best methods of securing the preservation of the order.

> Le gouvernement de l'ordre suppose des formes constitutives et nationales propres
> à chaque partie de l'administration pour la formation des loix nouvelles, pour la
> distribution de la justice, la hiérarchie, la compétence et le ressort des tribunaux
> . . . Seules les loix constitutives constituent un gouvernement régulier . . . ces loix,
> qui composent le second ordre des loix sociales . . . renferment les moyens que la
> société a pris pour assurer l'observation des premières loix, les préserver de toute
> atteinte et en réserver l'exécution à la société.[26]

Le Trosne's stand against the "contre-forces" that aim at opposing "une barrière au souverain, et de balancer son pouvoir"[27]
can be explained only by saying that his constitutional structure
did away with the necessity of a system of checks and balances,
which was necessary only where the legislative power had the right
"d'ériger en loix leurs volontés et de leur donner une forme
légale,"[28] and where the citizens could be seen to invoke "non des
principes immuables et essentiels, mais des loix positives auxquelles
le souverain déroge par la même autorité qui les a établies."[29]

Such would not be the case, however, in the physiocratic state,
where it was admitted that the power of making fundamental laws
belonged not to man but to God alone. Public opinion, finding its
articulate expression through the provincial assemblies and the
national council, would be quick to resent any attempt to violate
the rules of the order and would back the resistance which would
be put up by the courts.

> Ce seroit la nation entière qui réclameroit la justice clairement reconnue, et qui
> appuieroit la résistance des tribunaux et des corps intermédiaires de tout le poids de
> l'opinion publique. Et quelle force cette opinion unanime d'une nation éclairée ne
> donneroit-elle pas aux réclamations?[30]

For the first time we gather an explicit admission of the existence
of a power of control vested in the judiciary. And that the magistrates were the "guardians of the laws" is made clearer later on by
Le Trosne, who places them in an exalted position, at the same
time assigning them the highest duties.

[25] *De l'ordre*, p. 279. [27] *Ibid.*, p. 251. [29] *Ibid.*, p. 255.
[26] *Ibid.*, p. 278. [28] *Ibid.*, p. 253. [30] *Ibid.*, p. 259.

Les magistrats qui sont les dépositaires et les gardiens des loix, doivent avoir tout la connaissance explicite de la raison primitive et essentielle des loix, c'est-à-dire des loix fondamentales. Ils sont d'ailleurs le lien social qui unit le souverain avec les sujets: leur ministere forme une partie intégrale de la constitution de l'Etat; ils doivent donc connaître parfaitement cette constitution qui est la partie positive de l'ordre social. C'est à eux à donner l'exemple aux citoyens de cet attachement inviolable à la constitution qui fait la force morale de la société, et qui ajoute à la force physique un degré de force qui la rend indestructible. Enfin ils doivent être instruits des loix civiles, puisqu'ils sont chargés de les appliquer.[31]

The magistrates, then, by their devotion to the constitution, must be ready to preserve it against any attack or violation by the legislative power, rallying to their help the enlightened public opinion of the country.

Charles de Butré, who had remained on the sidelines until 1768, felt compelled to join the debate on the issue of judicial control once Mably had delivered a dangerous attack against the school in his *Doutes* of that year. In an article published in the *Ephémérides du citoyen*[32] he shows himself more realistic and practical than Le Mercier, whose exaggerated reliance upon the strength of the *évidence* of the laws of nature Butré disliked. It was possible for an enlightened public opinion to check ill-guided legislative trends, but, he adds, "Je ne croie pas facile de décider si elle seroit dans tous les cas capable de les arrêter. Il pourroit donc arriver que le despotisme légal tendît vers l'arbitraire, s'il n'avoit d'autre frein que l'évidence."[33] Evidence alone was not enough. For this reason the physiocratic school had added to it the strength of the judicial body charged with the verification of positive laws.

Et c'est pourquoi les Philosophes Economistes y ajoutent l'honneur et l'intérêt des Magistrats, qui ne sont point Législateurs, mais qui sont chargés de vérifier les Loix positives que le Souverain croit nécessaires, en les comparant avec les Loix naturelles de l'Ordre social. Le devoir que la conscience impose à ces Magistrats, le devoir négatif que leur donne l'évidence de la justice et de la raison, la nécessité que la conformité des Ordonnances nouvelles avec les Loix de la justice par essence soit constatée par leur examen, avant que ces Ordonnances puissent être mises à exécution; ont parus très propres à seconder, au milieu d'une Nation éclairée, le pouvoir de l'évidence: qui elle-même facilite aux Magistrats l'accomplissement des devoirs *essentiels* de leur ministere, et leur assure l'usage des *droits* respectables, qui leur sont confiés pour l'intérêt commun de la Nation et du Souverain.[34]

---

[31] *Ibid.*, p. 292.
[32] "Lettre de M. K. à M. le Chevalier de **. Au sujet des doutes de M. l'Abbé de Mably," (1768), VI, 128–165.
[33] "Lettre," *Ephémérides* (1768), VI, 163.
[34] "Lettre," *Ephémérides*, VI, 163–164.

In a subsequent work the direct influence of Quesnay is perhaps greater, and Butré's language is distinctly reminiscent of the founder's when he writes of the institution of magistrates "pour exercer les fonctions de la justice distributive." [35] But that is not their only duty, for they must compare "les ordonnances des souverains avec ces loix essentielles, dont elles ne doivent être que des conséquences évidentes." [36] Once more the principle of judicial control had been used to conclude a discussion of the political organization of the state.

Mably was also responsible for the addition of yet another name, La Vauguyon, to the list of expounders of the doctrine of judicial control. La Vauguyon's five articles in the *Ephémérides* are important in themselves and because they show both how widely accepted by the physiocratic school was the doctrine of judicial review and what central part it occupied in its political philosophy. La Vauguyon vigorously takes up with Mably the issue of control upon legislative acts. It is essential that there should be courts to compare positive with natural laws.

> Nous regardons, comme la base essentielle d'une administration éclairée, les Tribunaux qui décident, d'après les loix positives, des biens, de l'honneur et de la vie des Citoyens; et qui doivent être instruits des loix naturelles, de l'ordre social, pour comparer dans leur institution les loix positives de l'administration avec les loix naturelles et essentielles constitutives de tout Gouvernement.[37]

Whence is the power of such courts derived? It is true that Le Mercier did not endow them with any positive weapon, says La Vauguyon, who speaks on behalf of the entire school, but "ils les tiennent de Dieu ces moyens, et ils sont attachés à la sainteté de leurs fonctions, dirigées par l'évidence des loix naturelles de l'ordre de la Justice, auxquels toute la société bien instruite doit être soumise entièrement." [38] The function of the courts was to preserve the country from the mistakes and bad legislation to which it might have been subjected by an ill-guided legislative power that lay of necessity in the hands of the supreme ruler.

> Un seul homme peut être plus facilement surpris que plusieurs, qui dans l'admission d'une loi, ne sont pas exposés, comme le Législateur, à l'instigation de ceux qui sollicitent des loix injustes; et c'est aussi ce qui confirme la nécessité de ne jamais

---

[35] *Loix naturelles de l'agriculture et de l'ordre social* (Neuchâtel, 1781), p. 94.
[36] *Ibid.*
[37] Third letter, *Ephémérides* (1768), V, 238–239.
[38] *Ibid.*, p. 244.

rendre les Magistrats Législateurs, car alors les instigations s'adresseroient à eux, et la pluralité de leurs propres intérêts particuliers exclusifs susciteroit dans l'institution des loix, des factions, des complots, des intrigues redoutables et funestes à la société.[39]

Since Mably had suggested as possible the submission of the courts of review to the will of the legislative power, La Vauguyon paints the darkest possible picture of the consequences of such submission:

S'il était possible qu'un cas aussi malheureux arrivât, tout seroit alors en commotion. Le premier effet seroit l'alarme publique, et il seroit bientôt suivi de tous les excès qui peuvent naître d'une conduite si outrageante à l'égard d'une nation éclairée.[40]

Ignominy and disgrace would be heaped upon the heads of the magistrates who would have thus betrayed their trust. But that such a state of affairs can ever come about, as long as the nation at large is aware of the benefits of a strict observance of the law of nature, La Vauguyon hastens to deny.

Non . . . il n'est point d'intérêt, point de séduction, point de terreur, point de passion, qui puissent déterminer les Magistrats *instruits* d'un Peuple *instruit* à renoncer à la sainteté de leur auguste ministere, pour trainer ensuite des jours malheureux et détestés dans une situation aussi dure et aussi accablante. . . . Tant que les Magistrats seront éclairés, et que la lumière devenue générale, leur rappellera sans cesse l'importance des devoirs qu'ils ont à remplir dans la vérification des Loix positives; nous serons donc préservés de celles qui seroient décidées injustes par l'évidence: et son autorité invincible déterminera l'admission de celles qui seront reconnues sages et utiles.[41]

In brief, La Vauguyon suggests to his contemporary critic, in words that should have been carefully weighed by most of the later critics, that any appraisal of the political doctrine of the physiocrats should not comment lightly upon what constitutes one of its essential parts. Legal despotism should be judged in the light of the courts of legislative review. La Vauguyon is indignant that the critics of the school should fail to see this point. Addressing himself to Mably, he asks:

Pourquoi, Monsier, gardez-vous toujours le silence sur une condition essentielle de la législation dans les Monarchies: c'est le devoir des Tribunaux dans l'admission des loix? Ces Tribunaux chez une Nation éclairée, sont *nécessairement* instruits des Loix naturelles et constitutives; dont les loix positives de l'administration ne doivent être que des actes déclaratoires, revêtues d'une sanction qui assure d'autant plus l'obéissance que l'on doit à ces loix sacrées. Ce sont ces lumieres des Magistrats, c'est la fonction respectable d'en faire l'application dans l'examen préalable des nouvelles Loix positives qui s'opposent aux effets de la séduction et de la surprise dans le

[39] *Ibid.*, pp. 244–245.
[40] *Ibid.*, p. 245.
[41] *Ibid.*, pp. 247–248.

Souverain. Les Ordonnances que celui-ci promulgue, et a seul le droit de promulguer, ne deviennent exécutables, et ne forment proprement *des loix* qu'après qu'elles ont été *vérifiées* par les Magistrats.[42]

La Vauguyon, it is clear, followed closely the lines set down by Le Mercier. But the eloquence of his words and the finality and conviction with which the case is presented, had not been, and were not later, surpassed by any member of the school. It seems proper therefore to rescue La Vauguyon's name from the complete oblivion into which it had fallen.

We now come to Le Mercier, who has devoted more space than have any of his friends to the analysis of the power of the judges and of their functions in bringing about the realization of the natural order. He understood he had to start by making it clear beyond doubt that in order to carry out properly the duties entrusted to them the magistrates were to be independent of the legislative and executive bodies. Otherwise the certainty of justice was destroyed.[43] Despite the at times somewhat bewildering and contradictory language, one can discover that the reason for this is twofold, formal and substantive. Positive law must carry with it manifest proof that a certain procedural order has been followed in its preparation and issuance, in order to guarantee its justice and necessity. That this order has been followed there would be no longer any proof, were the legislative power to absorb the functions of the magistrates. Moreover, were the separation of the two powers not enforced, "si le législateur était aussi magistrat, il ne pourrait que couronner et consommer comme magistrat, toutes les méprises qui lui seraient echappées comme législateur." [44]

This second point is the more important, for it implies that, positive laws being but the declaration of the principles embodied in natural laws, power must reside somewhere to verify the compatibility of the former with the latter. That this power had to be entrusted to the judiciary Le Mercier on the whole makes clear. Judges have been throughout history the connecting link between the rulers and the ruled; they have always revealed the true significance of laws, have been the living embodiment of them. More, they are "éclairés par l'évidence *de la raison primitive et essentielle des*

[42] Fifth letter, *Ephémérides* (1768), VII, 192–193.
[43] *L'Ordre*, p. 63.
[44] *Ibid.*, p. 64.

lois." [45] They are "les dépositaires et gardiens des lois." Not that the appellation of "guardian of the law" is to be denied to the sovereign; rather, because of their functions, magistrates are "more particularly" so.

Now what all this entails is that judges must refuse themselves to enforce evidently unjust laws. No magistrate

peut se charger de juger d'après des loix *évidemment* injustes; il cesseroit alors d'être un ministre de la justice, pour devenir un ministre d'iniquité. Si quelque loi, par exemple, ordonnoit qu'un homme fût condamné au dernier supplice, sur la seule dénonciation d'un autre homme, et même sans aucune preuve de l'existence du délit imputé, n'est-il pas *évident* que telle loi seroit homicide? . . . Il faut pourtant ou aller jusqu'à dire qu'on pourroit être, sans crime, l'organe d'une telle loi, et le ministre de ses abominations, ou convenir qu'un magistrat ne doit prêter son ministère à aucune loi *évidemment* injuste.[46]

The possibility of the judge's distinguishing between what is just and what is unjust depends upon his knowledge of the principles of natural law, a knowledge that must perforce be assumed to be complete and thorough. "Qu'est-ce qui oblige un homme de se faire médecin, quand son ignorance l'expose à commettre journellement des assassinats?" Ignorance cannot thus be pleaded, the less so, since the foundations upon which rests the structure of natural law are extremely simple. Le Mercier sums them up in the words that, as we saw, had constituted the foundation of the school's economic theory and had paved the way for the construction of their political edifice: property and liberty. The defence of property and liberty must be the constant guiding criterion of action of the judges.

Une fois qu'on est pénétré da la justice et de la nécessité de ces deux loix divines; une fois que l'évidence de leur justice et de leur nécessité est publiquement répandue dans une nation, il n'est plus possible que la conformité ou la contradiction des nouvelles loix avec les principes immuables de l'ordre ne soient pas évidentes, non seulement pour le corps des magistrats, mais encore pour tous les hommes qui n'ont point perdu l'usage de la raison.[47]

The essential duties of the judges might then be thus set forth: in the first place, a knowledge of the principles of natural law and an understanding of the rational motives behind those positive laws which come up for enforcement.

Le magistrat est tenu d'avoir une connoissance *évidente* de la justice et de la nécessité des loix qu'il se charge *librement* de faire observer. Il ne lui est donc permis de

[45] *L'Ordre*, p. 69.
[46] *Ibid.*, p. 74.
[47] *Ibid.*, p. 75.

juger les hommes qu'après avoir pénétré scrupuleusement dans la raison des loix, et avoir acquis *l'évidence* de leur justice.[48]

The second inescapable duty, flowing directly from the acceptance of an order of law apart from and above that of positive law, is the refusal of the judge to consider enforcing laws of the positive order which conflict with those of that higher order of whose justice and necessity and superior validity he has become convinced. This is an "essential" obligation that can never be put aside; under no circumstances can the judge lend his offices to the enforcement of an unjust law. Then, and only then, will the people acquire the certainty that the laws they are called to obey are founded on reason and justice. It will not be possible

que le témoignage public qu'il [le magistrat] rend librement à la sagesse des loix nouvelles, ne soit pas regardé comme le résultat d'une *évidence* acquise par un examen suffisant . . . qu'un témoignage de cette importance, vérifié, pour ainsi dire, et contrôlé par la publicité des connoissances *évidentes* répandues dans la nation, n'établissent pas *nécessairement la certitude* de la justice et de la nécessité de ces mêmes loix dans tous ceux qui ne peuvent acquérir une connoissance évidente.[49]

One question has constantly presented itself to the minds of those who have, down to our day, attempted to appraise the consequences of this doctrine of judicial control upon the relative place within the frame of government of the judiciary and the legislative: will not the revisionary powers granted to the magistrates inevitably set them above the legislators whose duty it is to formulate laws, thus depriving them of all independence and of all real power? This same question is raised by Le Mercier: "Quelqu'un s'imaginera peut-être que les devoirs de la magistrature, tels que je les représente ici, sont destructifs du pouvoir législatif?" [50] And the answer he gives to it is entirely in the negative, as it only can be, when the nature of legislative functions according to the physiocratic school is remembered. For Le Mercier a true perspective of the powers of the legislative body will reveal how little is left to its imaginative faculties and how much to its interpretative ones: "Le pouvoir législatif n'est . . . autre chose que le pouvoir d'annoncer des loix déjà faites nécessairement, et de les armer d'une force coercitive." [51] The verification of legislative actions by a judicial body does not imply any superiority of the former over the latter; rather, it implies the subordination of both to a higher

[48] *L'Ordre*, p. 75.
[49] *Ibid.*, p. 76.

[50] *Ibid.*, p. 85.
[51] *Ibid.*, p. 82.

natural order whose "evident" necessity and intrinsic justice have already been made apparent to the society of men.

Il est donc certain que les devoirs des magistrats sont entièrement à l'avantage de l'autorité législative dans une nation instruite telle que nous la supposons. Cette autorité, dont les intérêts personnels sont en tout point les mêmes que ceux de la nation, n'a rien à craindre que les méprises; et de-là nous pouvons juger combien doit lui être util et précieux un corps de citoyens institués pour être, plus particulièrement encore que tous les autres dépositaires et gardiens de l'évidence même; qui en cette qualité sont chargés de veiller sans cesse autour de l'autorité législative; de placer toujours entre elle et la mauvaise volonté des hommes ignorants ou mal intentionnés, le bouclier impénétrable de l'évidence.[52]

Even the argument based on the historical experience of mankind, that magistrates have never constituted very formidable barriers against the inroads of a tyrannical legislative power, are brushed aside by Le Mercier with the remark that countries so afflicted were still completely ignorant of the "order" of permanent values which had now been discovered.[53]

Throughout this discussion of the relationship between the magistrates and the legislative power, it may be observed, Le Mercier shows sympathy for the legislator who, according to him can only be "misled" into approving something which he at heart must condemn. The purity of the motives of the legislative body cannot be challenged in a commonwealth where the "order" rules; and the duty of the magistrates is not to prevent a band of sinners from getting away unpunished with their crimes; rather, it is to remedy the slips inadvertently committed by well-meaning souls fully convinced of their subordinate position.

Dupont was very conscious of what he thought was the great change that the physiocratic doctrine had wrought in the political outlook of the country. What was held valid a few years earlier was no longer so, now that the existence of the natural order had been ascertained. Montesquieu himself could not escape Dupont's criticism, for had he not maintained that the principles of government must change according to the constitution? This relativity had no place in a world that had come to believe in Quesnay, Gournay, Mirabeau, and Le Mercier, and in their system of permanent political order, which could not be changed and to which it was the imperative duty of the princes to give expression.[54] The

[52] *L'Ordre*, p. 87.
[53] *Ibid.*, p. 89.
[54] Dupont, *De l'origine*, p. 7.

foundation of this order was the landowner; its aim, the attainment of the greatest happiness through the highest possible development of the agricultural net product. Property, liberty, and security — these were the ideals to be secured through a sovereign authority, where all power that could be entrusted to man was to reside.

L'idée de plusieurs autorités dans un même État, ne présente qu'une absurdité complette. Si elles sont égales, il n'y a point d'autorité; il ne peut y avoir que plus ou moins d'anarchie. Si l'une d'entre elles est supérieure, celle-là est l'autorité; les autres ne sont rien.[55]

If Dupont was willing to accept the traditional physiocratic "despot," even though he refrained from calling him such,[56] it was because Dupont knew what a limited amount of power was to be entrusted to the despot.

L'autorité souveraine n'est pas instituée pour *faire des loix*: car *les loix sont toutes faites* par la main de celui qui créa *les droits et les devoirs.* . . . Les Ordonnances des Souverains qu'on appelle *loix positives,* ne doivent être que des *actes déclaratoires de ces loix essentielles de l'ordre social.*[57]

And there existed a natural and irrefutable test of these manmade laws: it was their conformity with, or opposition to, the natural laws of the social order. The problem of who was to undertake this test is solved by Dupont in what had become by now the orthodox physiocratic doctrine. The judicial guarantee is accepted as an integral part of the system of government. While executive and legislative powers were to be one, a separate judicial establishment was necessary, to be given the task of supervising and controlling the lawmaking activities of the sovereign:

Les magistrats étant chargés de juger d'après les loix positives, et conformément aux règles prescrites par les loix positives; et ayant à décider ainsi des biens, de la

[55] *De l'origine,* p. 16.

[56] Schelle (*Du Pont,* pp. 177–179) makes a good deal out of Dupont's refusal in 1775, when publishing his *Table raisonnée des principes d'économie politique,* to use any more the words *legal despotism,* which had been so damaging to the school, and of his yielding to Turgot's insistence that he substitute for *autorité tutélaire,* which he wished to use, the words *autorité publique.* This would appear to Schelle the final proof that Dupont had thus broken the chain which had bound him to Quesnay's autocratic doctrines, and had reverted to his original liberal principles. This interpretation springs from a misunderstanding of the concept of legal despotism. The truth is that Quesnay's so-called despotism was highly qualified by various guarantees, and that Dupont had accepted, and to the end of his life believed in, the substance of the economic and political doctrines of Quesnay, whatever the words he used to define them (see, for instance, Jefferson's letter, below, p. 84).

[57] *De l'origine,* p. 16.

vie, de l'honneur de leurs concitoyens; ils sont religieusement obligés de commencer par juger les loix positives. Il est évident qu'un magistrat serait coupable, qui se chargerait de prononcer des peines contre ses semblables d'après des loix *évidemment injustes*. Les Magistrats doivent donc comparer les Ordonnances positives avec les Loix de la *Justice par essence*, qui règlent les droits et les devoirs de chacun et qui sont ainsi la base de l'ordre social, avant de s'engager à juger d'après ces Ordonnances.[58]

The sovereign power itself, if in the hands of an hereditary monarch free from the pressure of local and temporary interests, will solicit and pray for this test of the validity of positive laws; usually the issue would be clear-cut, and the law would be either wholly accepted or wholly rejected. An independent body of judges, then, is one of the greatest needs of a commonwealth: "pour décider dans les cas particuliers quelle doit être l'application des loix de l'ordre naturel, réduites en loix positives par l'autorité souveraine; et qui ont le devoir impérieux de comparer les Ordonnances des Souverains avec les loix de la Justice par essence." [59]

Dupont gives judicial control great emphasis, even though he leaves somewhat in the air both the procedure to be followed and the consequences of an adverse opinion of the judiciary. To Dupont's mind, perhaps, the consequences of judicial action need not be dwelt upon. The law in question, if rejected by the bench, was to lose validity. But he attempted, in an introductory essay to the *Physiocratie*, which belongs to the end of 1767, to clear up the first point. The essay contains also a restatement in general terms of the whole doctrine, with an appeal to the judiciary to learn the principles of the new science, since these afforded the best guide for the accomplishment of their duty.

Organes et Dépositaires des Loix, Magistrats respectables, elle est faite pour vous cette science. Vous ne sauriez sans crime vous dispenser de la posséder à fond. Vous avez à decider de la fortune, de la vie, de l'honneur de vos Concitoyens. . . . Comment rempliriez-vous cette fonction indispensable et sainte, si vous ignoriez quelles sont les loix de l'ordre que Dieu a établi pour servir de règles à la société? La science de ces Loix est donc essentielle à votre ministere. Si elle était malheureusement bannie du reste du globe, ce serait chez vous qu'elle devrait se refugier. Par elle seule vous pouvez assurer la soumission et le respect des Peuples aux Loix que promulgue le Souverain. Par elle seule vous pouvez tranquilliser le Souverain même en lui garantissant la sagesse et l'utilité de ses Ordonnances.[60]

The task of reviewing positive legislation was a duty not to be skirted.

[58] *Ibid.*, p. 18.
[59] *Ibid.*, p. 34.
[60] *Physiocratie*, I, lxxxi, lxxxv.

Mais vous rendriez compte à celui qui fit la Justice, si vous vous engagiez imprudemment à régler vos décisions par des Ordonnances contraires à l'équité, et attentatoires aux droits de l'homme. Avant de juger vos frères, vous êtes donc strictement et religieusement obligés de juger les Loix; et vous le faites. Les Ordonnances, évidemment absurdes, évidemment injustes, sont comme non-avenues pour vous.[61]

The judges should not attempt to dodge the issue confronting them by relying on the lapse of time to bring about a correction of legislative wrongs.

La désuetude est un remede illégal et tardif aux mauvaises Loix. Malheur aux Magistrats indignes qui croiraient pouvoir décharger leur conscience sur l'espoir de ce remede honteux et lent, dont l'application paraîtra toujours arbitraire au Peuple mal instruit, et compromettra par conséquent toujours l'honneur de la Magistrature.[62]

[61] *Physiocratie*, I, lxxxii.
[62] *Ibid.*, I, lxxxiii–lxxxiv.

CHAPTER VI

WAYS AND LIMITS OF JUDICIAL CONTROL

1. The Precedent of Parliament

IN THEIR affirmation of principle it is thus clear that the physiocrats were anxious to establish a judicial control whose decisions were not to be submitted to any authority in a position to overrule them. The magistrates were supreme, and the prince had to bow before them. How did the physiocrats propose in practice to go about the business of establishing this control? Could they rely on any precedent to guide them, and, if so, how did this precedent react on their subsequent interpretation and application of the doctrine?

There is no doubt that the precedent to which they more or less consciously had turned from the beginning was that of the parliaments of their own country. To the parliamentary tradition, moreover, public opinion for good or for ill linked their activities; so that, before we proceed with a further analysis of the school's thought, we have to consider briefly the substance and the implications of the parallel between the parliamentary and the physiocratic doctrines of control.

As already stated, the public mind quickly associated the type of control advocated by Le Mercier and his friends with the control which the parliament had tried to win over the royal power. Was there any real ground, however, for such an association? We do not believe that the physiocratic doctrine of judicial control was born under the wings of the parliamentary system, since it ignored the most significant feature of that system, the *lits de justice*, which usually terminated any real attempt at resistance. Could the Paris parliament at the middle of the eighteenth century have fired the imagination of Quesnay and his followers by any instance of defense of the kingdom's fundamental laws? This can hardly be true.

Far from being influenced by the parliamentary doctrine of remonstrance, the physiocrats had been struck by the futility to which the Paris parliament especially had sunk and by the use to which the *lits de justice* had been turned.

There is no doubt that, at a time when legislative and judiciary functions were hardly separated because hardly different, and when they consisted in law-declaring rather than in lawmaking, medieval doctrine recognized the right of parliaments to proclaim void royal statutes contrary to reason or fundamental law.[1] This doctrine applied to France as well as to England. Then the Paris parliament shared with the king whatever legislative power he had been able to gain for himself, and that was not much. But the situation changed entirely as soon as, with the beginning of the fourteenth century, the separation of judiciary and legislative powers, that is, the separation between the *Parlement* and the *Grand Conseil*, became apparent. For at first, and until the middle of the sixteenth century, that right of control was forgotten; when it was revived, it remained nothing more than an aspiration, most of the time a subconscious aspiration.

The Paris parliament never claimed a real control of the king's actions in the last four or five hundred years of its existence. It did claim that power to ultimate control of legislative acts in May 1788, but then the Paris parliament was already dead. Their words are as follows:

> Que la monarchie est gouvernée par le roi suivant les lois, que de ces lois plusieurs sont fondamentales . . . et embrassent et consacrent . . . le droit des Cours de vérifier dans chaque province les volontés du roi, et de n'en ordonner l'enregistrement qu'autant qu'elles sont conformes aux lois constitutives de la province ainsi qu'aux lois fondamentales.[2]

The last words are, of course, the most important. It would be interesting to know how many times they had been uttered before. But they never constituted the basis of the court's actions.

Parliament did not claim and the kings did not grant any control over their legislative activities, once they had succeeded in increasing their jurisdiction at the expense of the feudal lords,[3] even

---

[1] Charles H. McIlwain, *The High Court of Parliament* (New Haven, 1910), pp. 271–272.

[2] Petiet, *Du pouvoir législatif en France* (Paris, 1891), p. 222. This *arrêt* is not to be found in Flammermont.

[3] Cf. the answer given by Charles IX to the Paris parliament in 1563: "Les roys mes prédécesseurs ne vous ont mis en lieu où vous estes tous pour estre les tuteurs ni protecteurs du royaume. . . . Et ne vous veux plus laisser en erreur, mais vous commande de ne vous mesler que de la justice. Et quand je vous commanderai quelque chose, si y trouvez aucune difficulté pour l'entendre, je trouverai toujours bon que vous m'en faciez remontrance . . . et ayans ouï ma volonté, sans plus de replique y obéir" (Isambert, *Recueil général des anciennes lois françaises* [Paris, 1823–1833], XIV, 142–143). Also the *Ordonnance* of 1566: "Les ordonnances par nous faites . . . seront gardées et observées en nos parlemens, grand conseil, chambre des comptes . . . nonobstant les remontrances faites ou réservées à faire sur aucun

though they had granted such control when the great vassals, not
they, were the masters.[4]

What were, then, the functions of the Paris parliament in the
centuries that immediately followed its establishment primarily
as a court of justice? By its new composition, which practically
excluded any representation of feudal origin, the parliament's chief
function was not the control but the furtherance and expansion
of the royal power and the process of centralization and unification
of the kingdom. "Ça été le Parlement qui nous a sauvés d'être
cantonnés et démembrés comme en Italie et en Allemagne et qui a
maintenu le royaume en son entier."[5] Loyseau's words, written at
the very beginning of the seventeenth century, epitomize the work
of parliament during the three preceding centuries. The first use,
in 1392, of the privilege of remonstrance was prompted not by the
desire of parliament to limit the royal power, but by a belief that
the king had neglected sufficiently to assert his jurisdiction.[6] The
same is true of the more famous remonstrance caused by the abolition of the Pragmatic Sanction in 1461. It may be added that of
course when the parliament upheld the king in his fight against
vassals and church it did so to save the crown, not the man who
happened to be its wearer. Through the crown the parliament was
anxious to protect the nation. But historically the consequence was
to determine a quick disappearance of all effective parliamentary
power.

It is true that, confronted in the sixteenth century with an increasing royal power, the Paris parliament attempted to vindicate
its rights. But what were those rights? Did they include the power
of declaring void a royal edict? It does not seem so. Notwithstanding the theoretical claims of such lawyers as Guy de Coquille,

---

articles d'icelles, nonobstant aussi que nos édits et ordonnances n'ayent esté publiées
en aucune desdites cours" (Isambert, *Recueil général*, XIV, 190). This *Ordonnance*
proves that not even the formal right of registration was exclusive to the parliaments or, then, necessary for the validity of the law (cf. also Petiet, *Du pouvoir
législatif*, p. 169).

[4] "Si les lettres du Prince ne sont conformes à la justice et à la raison, si elles
contrarient ou contreviennent aux ordonnances, si elles déclinent de l'ordre et
ancienne observance d'icelles, ou y dérogent en tout ou partie, ils [les parlements]
doivent les déclarer nulles, injustes ou subreptices." From a fourteenth-century royal
ordinance, recalled by the Paris parliament in its remonstrance of November 27,
1755 (cf. Jules Flammermont and Maurice Tourneux, *Remontrances du Parlement
de Paris au XVIIIe siècle*, Paris, 1888–98, II, 33).

[5] Charles Loyseau, *Traité des seigneuries* (Paris, 1608), chap. V.

[6] Cf. Petiet, *Du pouvoir législatif*, p. 170.

the powers were in practice limited to the rights of registration and remonstrance, two rights which have very little to do with the power of control.[7] Proof is to be found on all sides that parliament was anxious to preserve above all the right of registration, because it believed that right an indispensable link in the procedural process which gave formal validity to a law. Form rather than substance appears to be parliament's motive in one of the most famous of its statements of the issue. The laws of the kingdom, says the parliament of Paris in 1641,

sont immortelles, et ne peuvent être changées, variées ni altérées, pour quelque cause que ce soit. Entre ces dernières il y en a une certaine et inviolable, savoir qu'une loi n'est point réputée loi, ni une ordonnance tenue pour une ordonnance, qu'elle n'ait été apportée en ce lieu, qui est le *consistoire* des rois et du royaume, délibérée, publiée, et registrée." [8]

Throughout the seventeenth and eighteenth centuries the chief complaints of the various parliaments centered upon the loss of jurisdiction to other courts, the allocation to the Grand Conseil of business which had been traditionally theirs.[9] Even though the belief existed that the *lits de justice* were a usurpation, nothing was done to check their increased use by the kings since the sixteenth century for the purposes of breaking down the parliaments' occasionally stubborn resistance. Only the words "following express commandment of the king" would be inserted at the end of the act of registration of the law at issue. And when once, in the middle of the seventeenth century, at the height of parliamentary power, the Paris parliament dared to question the constitutional validity of a royal edict registered in *lit de justice*, the stupefaction was great on both sides. Parliament thereupon quickly withdrew from its unheard-of position.[10]

It was, then, a parliament deprived of any real power of control of legislative actions which the physiocrats contemplated in their time. The last hundred years of the history of the Paris parliament, from the death of Mazarin in 1661 to the great remonstrances of 1755, had seen the slow debasement of its authority,

[7] Cf. Kingsley Martin, *French Liberal Thought in the XVIIIth Century* (London and Boston, 1929), p. 84.

[8] Cf. Petiet, *Du pouvoir législatif*, pp. 215–216.

[9] Cf. the already mentioned remonstrance of November 27, 1755 (Flammermont, *Remontrances*, II, 12 ff.), which represents the greatest effort accomplished by the Paris parliament in the eighteenth century in defense of its own rights.

[10] Cf. Paul Rice Doolin, *The Fronde* (Cambridge, 1935), p. 63, and Petiet, *Du pouvoir législatif*, p. 217.

the almost complete abandonment of the exercise of the right of
remonstrance, the use by the king, on the slightest pretext, of the
weapon of the *lit de justice*. A new spirit seemed to arise in the
middle of the eighteenth century. The remonstrances of 1755, with
their learned if specious restatement of the essential function of
parliament in preserving the constitution of France,[11] are a proof
of it. The revival was short-lived, and it can be said that during
the last 150 years of its existence Parliament never did succeed
in either checking for any appreciable period, or getting the best
of, the royal power, however paralyzing that body's efforts might
have proved to be at the time of its greatest power.[12]

The great glories of the Paris parliament had been the administration of justice, the coördination of the *droit coûtumier*, and the
enactment of administrative acts in many important fields. The
monarchy did not allow parliament to share its legislative powers,
and the recourse to the *lits de justice* struck at the very root of the
idea of judicial control. And, if we take into account only the
formal declarations of parliament, it had never been imagined, except once in 1648 and again at the very end,[13] that a royal edict,
registered only under the king's express will in the course of a *lit
de justice*, should not be deemed perfectly valid from a constitutional point of view. There is no doubt that the significance of the
parliament's work had been essentially moral and that the import
both of its privileges of registration and of remonstrance was, in
the last analysis, a merely formal one, because of the admittedly
overriding powers of the king. It was precisely on this point that
the physiocratic doctrine made the greatest advance over the traditional parliamentary doctrine, by granting a final power of decision to the magistrates.

The physiocratic school had, besides, no reason to be grateful
for the Paris parliament's attitude towards the several reforms attempted by Turgot. The parliament's opposition helped to wreck
the first considerate and coördinated effort to put through the phys-

[11] See the text in Flammermont, *Remontrances*, II, 12–107. The parliament had
taken as its guide the work of Louis-Adrien Lepaige, *Lettres historiques sur les fonctions essentielles du Parlement, sur le droit des Pairs, et sur les loix fondamentales du
Royaume* (Paris, 1753–54), 2 volumes.

[12] Cf. Ennamond Fayard, *Aperçu historique sur le Parlement de Paris* (Paris,
1878), III, 471 ff.

[13] Cf. Ernest Glasson, *Le Parlement de Paris. Son rôle politique* (Paris, 1901),
II, 446, and above, p. 48.

iocratic economic platform. The failure of Turgot in 1776 ended whatever influence the physiocratic school still retained. This failure may explain why, when the possibility of calling together a popular assembly dawned upon the political horizon of France, Dupont had no doubt that such an assembly would be a better positive instrument of action than a hypothetical negative resistance offered by the courts to a royal power reluctant to carry out the seemingly fantastic program of the physiocratic school. Dupont subordinated his adhesion to judicial control to the possibility of obtaining through it the fulfillment of certain ideals, primarily economic.

Of course the physiocratic doctrine of judicial control owes its origin to the same principle which had remained the aspiration of parliament and which had been its ultimate but unrealized aim during many centuries: the belief in certain immutable laws which had to be protected against sudden and ill-considered alterations. While parliament appealed to fundamental laws essentially historical in their nature and representing the specific tradition of France, the physiocrats, in their first group of writings at least, based their appeal on natural laws, rational in character, although conceived in terms particularly fitted to the needs of the country. But, and this is the crucial point, the physiocratic school attempted to go beyond the point reached by parliament. It met a royal power, moderate and constitutional, it is true, in its assertions of authority, but one which admitted no challenge from the parliamentary quarter. Against such a tradition of royal supremacy not even a judicial control made less apparent by the shadow of legal despotism could make headway.

This very fiction of legal despotism was, moreover, one of the causes of the unpopularity and downfall of the physiocratic doctrine of control. Too much emphasis had been given by the physiocrats to their criticism of the system of checks and balances, a system which in reality they did their best to establish through the essentially identical system of guarantees. The inevitable result was to make doubtful in the public eyes the sincerity of the espousal of the doctrine of judicial control, which, in order to acquire any real significance, needed as its starting point the existence of the hotly combatted system of checks and balances.

Also, it may be added, the type of judicial control advanced by the school was wrongly identified by the country with the control exercised by the Paris parliament, or for that matter, by all French parliaments, over the king's use of legislative and executive functions, that is, with the working of an institution which had never been able to exercise a real control over the royal power. And if we assume the reception accorded to any one theory to be based upon its conceivable usefulness, then we should not wonder at the fate meted to the doctrine of judicial control the moment it became associated in the popular mind with the Paris parliament.

2. THE CONSTITUTIONAL PLACE OF JUDICIAL CONTROL ACCORDING TO LE MERCIER

In accordance with the general tenor of his work, Le Mercier adheres in his *Ordre* to a strictly abstract treatment of the problem. No mention is made of the point at which this judicial control is to take place, although we may perhaps infer that it is to occur in a preliminary stage, when the law is not yet promulgated and the judges act in an advisory capacity, rather than at a later period, when the law is being opposed before the courts by wounded private interests.[14] What is to be defended is an abstract order whose component parts he called liberty and property. No definite effort had yet been made by 1767 to bring forward a concrete system of reforms. In 1772 Le Mercier states that in every political body with claims to life there always exists "des loix immuables et fondamentales, des loix que le Souverain sera dans l'heureuse impuissance de changer." [15] And in 1775 he repeats that every society must have "des loix fondamentales et invariables, auxquelles par conséquent ce législateur ne puisse absolument déroger." [16]

But just as in America the revolution and the subsequent emergence of a new political order based on a written constitution provided the ground for a shift in the treatment of judicial review from a primarily rational and abstract basis to a constitutional one, so in France the revolution caused Le Mercier to abandon his appeals to an unwritten code of nature as the law to be enforced by the judiciary. Written constitutions were to be considered as the living embodiment of that code, the compatibility with their clauses the supreme test to which ordinary laws had to be submitted.

Le Mercier's terminology is changed. His doctrine remains the

[14] *L'Ordre*, pp. 148 ff.
[15] *Lettre sur les économistes* (2nd ed.; Paris, 1787), p. 73. Reprinted fifteen years after its original appearance, as an answer against the criticisms of Mallet du Pan.
[16] *Nouvelles Éphémérides économiques* (Paris, 1775), X, 116, note.

same. We find it in three essays, written between 1788 and 1792, one of them very voluminous, all of them less well-known than his *Ordre*.[17]

We are confronted at the outset with a distinction between constitutional order and administrative order, rather than with a distinction between natural and positive law. From this distinction two essentially different types of law necessarily emerge: the constitutional or fundamental laws, and the administrative or ordinary laws.

De cette distinction nous voyons naître deux sortes de loix: d'abord, les loix de la constitution, connues parmis nous sous le nom de loix fondamentales, loix nécessairement immuables, puisqu'elles sont les titres communs du monarque et de ses sujets; ensuite, les loix de l'administration, qui sont nécessairement variables, parce qu'elles sont toujours dépendantes des changemens successifs, auxquels se trouvent naturellement assujettis les objets qui sont de leur ressort. . . . Une conséquence bien naturelle et bien importante à tirer de ces premières vérités, c'est que les loix de l'administration ne doivent jamais se trouver destructives de la constitution: en deux mots, l'administration ne doit être que le développement et l'application des loix de la constitution, ou, pour mieux dire, que la constitution même mise en exécution.[18]

While the administrative laws should always be "registered" by the appropriate controlling bodies, even if the latter do not find themselves in agreement with the contents of the laws submitted to their approval, this should never happen with acts that do not merely declare what the law is but that create it. These are the laws which Le Mercier calls constitutional, giving perhaps to the word a wider significance than it usually has. This is made clear by the procedure which, he explains, applies to normal, not to revolutionary, times, or to times when the States General are convoked.

The king, who is the supreme legislative power, needs an advisory body specially charged with the important duty of verifying the constitutionality of new laws. Usually, Le Mercier believes, the king and the members of this body would agree on what is constitutional and what is not. But the possibility of a disagreement has to be considered.

Supposons-les pour un moment d'avis absolument contraires; qu'en resultera-t-il? Que si le monarque persiste, l'enregistrement qu'il aura ordonné, doit avoir lieu, et procurer à sa loi nouvelle une exécution provisoire, en attendant qu'une assemblée

---

[17] *Les Voeux d'un Français, ou considérations sur les principaux objets dont le Roi et la Nation vont s'occuper* (Paris, 1788); *Essais sur les maximes et loix fondamentales de la Monarchie française, ou Canevas d'un code constitutionnel* (Paris, 1789); *L'Heureuse Nation ou relations du gouvernement des féliciens, peuple souverainement libre sous l'empire absolu des loix* (Paris, 1792), 2 volumes.

[18] *Les Voeux*, pp. 33–35.

nationale puisse lui faire connoître le voeux general de la nation, relativement à cette loi.[19]

But, as already pointed out, constitutional laws should not be given even this temporary validity. Le Mercier's words in this respect contain in a nutshell the essence of his theory.

Il est à remarquer encore que cette exécution provisoire, qui, dans le système monarchique, doit être accordée aux volontés du souverain, ne peut s'appliquer qu'aux loix nouvelles concernant l'administration, puisque ce sont les seules qui soient du ressort de sa puissance législatrice. Si donc on lui en suggéroit quelqu'une qui se trouvât incompatible avec la constitution, les officiers publics chargés de la vérification et de l'enregistrement des loix nouvelles, ne pourroient consentir à l'enregistrer, quelque formels que fussent les ordres qu'ils recevroient à cet égard. La raison en est sensible: la puissance législatrice du monarque ne s'étend point sur la constitution, ne lui donne point le pouvoir de faire des loix destructives de la constitution: or, des loix que la constitution ne permet pas au monarque d'instituer, sont certainement des loix qu'elle ne permet pas non plus à ses officiers publics d'enregistrer.[20]

Having established this fundamental principle in clear terms, Le Mercier proceeds to consider the nature of the body he has empowered to pass upon the constitutionality of laws. After a new definition of what he means by "vérification" ("Vérifier une nouvelle loi, c'est la comparer, la combiner avec les anciennes, et principalement avec celles de la constitution; c'est examiner si elle leur est conséquente ou contraire; l'enregistrer, c'est la placer dans les régistres où les loix sont inscrites"),[21] Le Mercier is led to conclude that this process has of necessity a judicial character and that, therefore, those to whom it is entrusted should belong to a specially trained body of judges.

Le résultat de la vérification est un véritable jugement, qui, comme tous les autres jugemens, ne peut être dicté que par la conscience de ceux qui sont préposés pour le rendre. De telles fonctions requièrent des hommes accoutumés à se pénétrer de l'esprit et de l'intention des loix; elles sont une véritable magistrature; et comme elles intéressent également le souverain et toute la nation, il est clair qu'elles doivent naturellement être exercées par les magistrats supérieurs.[22]

The fact that Le Mercier believed that the revision of laws should be a primary, specific, and not merely an incidental function, explains why he thought it proper to avoid conflicting interpretations, to restrict revision to the highest judges of the country. Whether these judges should sit in one or more courts Le Mercier

[19] *Les Voeux*, p. 39.
[20] *Ibid.*, pp. 40–41.
[21] *Ibid.*, p. 52. The terms are the familiar ones used by the parliaments. But the power which Le Mercier gives to his judges is much more real.
[22] *Ibid.*, pp. 52–53.

does not explain at this point. His words are of a general character, referring merely to functions of revision to be exercised by high magistrates. But that he was thinking of the Paris parliament as the place where the high magistrates capable of performing that job were to be found is made clear beyond question by the entire content of the book. He was himself a member of that parliament, and it was difficult for him to escape the influence of the atmosphere by which he was surrounded. And it was entirely natural that French monarchical writers who summed up in the king all legislative and executive powers should turn to the parliament, with its not entirely earned tradition of struggle with the royal prerogative behind it, once they had discovered the existence of certain fundamental law which could not be violated and which needed protection. There was no necessity to create new bodies; indeed, "ce corps étoit déjà tout trouvé, tout institué; il existoit dans celui qui, depuis la fondation de la monarchie, avoit toujours été le conseil législatif de nos monarques." [23] But of course Le Mercier was endowing the Paris parliament with powers which only some of its interpreters had theoretically claimed for it; for while no parliament had ever refused ultimately to comply with the king's will, Le Mercier was anxious to set it up as an insuperable barrier against despotism and to have the king yield to the parliament's decisions. Refuting the notion that thus parliament would be called to share the legislative power with the king, Le Mercier explains the nature of the work accomplished by parliament in the past:

> On ne partage véritablement une autorité, que quand on est pleinement libre de consentir ou de ne pas consentir, de vouloir ou de ne pas vouloir ce qu'elle propose. Mais sur l'article de la vérification des loix, le parlement ne jouissoit pas d'une semblable liberté. Cette vérification, comme on l'a déjà vu, n'étoit qu'un examen nécessaire pour parvenir à rendre un jugement; et jamais un jugement ne fut un acte libre de la volonté. Ceux qui étoient chargés de le rendre, en cela n'exerçoient point *un droit*; ils ne faisoient que remplir *un devoir* resultant de la nature des choses, et à eux recommandé par nos rois mêmes.[24]

The doctrine of judicial control is thus expounded by Le Mercier with a clarity and a logical vigor not found in his former work: a king, supreme, but not endowed with tyrannical power; an assembly to regulate taxation, control expenditures, and "éclairer le prince sur tout ce qui concerne l'intérêt commun"; property,

[23] *Les Voeux*, p. 87.
[24] *Ibid.*, pp. 88–89.

liberty, and justice guaranteed to all; these principles and this organization

clearly established in a code of fundamental laws, immutable and not to be changed without the consent of the nation. The guardianship of these immutable laws to be entrusted to a body of magistrates, bound never to lend their help to novelties destructive of this monarchical constitution. New laws, therefore, to be submitted to a control which must be freely undertaken by these magistrates, in order to decide whether, according to the best of their judgment, they are not incompatible with those fundamental laws, to the conservation of which they are dedicated.[25]

In the shift from a philosophical to a constitutional platform Le Mercier was anxious to put down his ideas within the rigid frame of a constitutional project. The *Canevas d'un code constitutionnel* was Le Mercier's contribution to the revolutionary demand for a new instrument of government. After an introductory essay we find the text of the proposed constitution divided into titles and articles. Article III of title IV sets forth that the powers of the legislative bodies are subordinate and find their ultimate limitation in those fundamental laws established by the nation:

Les loix délibérées par la nation et sanctionnées par son chef, ne peuvent être ni abrogées, ni changées, par le pouvoir législatif établi pour la representer: l'institution de ce pouvoir n'a d'autre objet que d'assurer l'exécution de ces mêmes loix, par les développemens et les applications de leurs conséquences.[26]

(The strict dependence of the legislative power on the constitution was even more emphatically propounded three years later in Le Mercier's last work, *L'Heureuse Nation*,[27] as he recognized in this principle the keystone of his entire political structure.) Le Mercier was following a familiar path. Articles IV and V are devoted to an explanation of the difference existing between constitutional and administrative laws. The former are the basis of the political edifice, determining the nature and form of the government and guaranteeing the permanence of monarchical rule: "De

[25] *Ibid.*, pp. 55–56.
[26] *Canevas*, p. 18.
[27] "Je ne puis donc raisonablement vous parler du Pouvoir Législatif, qu'en le considérant dans une Société formée par une Constitution, et comme étant une des institutions *essentieles* de cette société: cela posé, je vous dirai que bien loin d'y figurer comme un Pouvoir indépendant de la Constitution, il doit lui être entièrement subordoné, atendu que c'est d'elle qu'il tient toute son Autorité; que jamais elle n'a entendu ni pu entendre lui donner le pouvoir de la détruire; qu'elle ne l'a même institué, que pour trouver en lui un Organe et un Défenseur: s'il étoit libre au Pouvoir Législatif de changer la Constitution, il n'y auroit point de Constitution; et s'il n'y avoit point de Constitution, il n'y auroit point de Pouvoir Législatif, parce qu'il n'y auroit point de Société (*L'Heureuse Nation*, II, 402–403).

telles loix sont nécessairement immuables; et la nation même ne pourroit les changer, sans dénaturer la monarchie." [28]   The latter are but a reflection of the "mouvemens journaliers du corps politique, et servent à les diriger suivant les circonstances éventuelles auxquelles ils correspondent." This being the case, administrative laws are bound to change correspondingly, "sans néanmoins pouvoir jamais être contraires, ni aux loix de la constitution, ni aux autres loix délibérées dans les assemblées nationales." [29]

This distinction defined the sphere of action reserved to the legislative body: it should tread carefully upon the field of administrative laws, while refraining entirely from even approaching that of constitutional law: "Les objets d'administration seront les seuls sur lesquels pourra s'exercer l'autorité de la puissance législatrice instituée par la nation." [30]   And it led to the conclusion that in order to enforce the distinction and to guarantee the sacredness of constitutional laws a special body was required. The conditions and consequences of its acting and its procedure were given in article II of title V. Again the separation of these functions of control from the legislative power and their judicial nature are emphasized.[31] Since it is the duty of the magistrates to give meaning and reality to the law, it is also their duty, their highest, to decide what does or does not constitute a valid expression of the legislative will.

If we look at Le Mercier's writings over a period of twenty-five years we are able to notice the coherence of his thought concerning that problem which was uppermost in his mind: how to achieve a stable political order through a constant adherence to a fundamental law. The problem was first pressed upon him when he was confronted with the necessity of guaranteeing the success of the theoretical structure, primarily economic, erected by his master Quesnay. He solved it first with a system of guarantees expressed in terms of natural law. When called upon later by the emergence of the revolutionary tide to produce a practicable plan of reform, he perceived the necessity of changing a philosophical theory into a precise formula of constitutional government. He did so with ability and courage. He elaborated the distinction between fundamental and administrative law, and he expounded the theory of judicial control in a way not surpassed by any member of the

[28] *Canevas*, p. 20.
[29] *Ibid.*
[30] *Ibid.*
[31] Articles III and IV of title V, *Canevas*, pp. 23–24.

physiocratic school. Unlike many of his friends, he was not dislodged from his position by the changing political scene; and he attempted with the use of a new phraseology to secure the success of his old ideal of the rule of the law of nature.

3. DUPONT AND HIS ABANDONMENT OF JUDICIAL CONTROL

No prolonged discussion of the point at which judicial control is to take effect is to be found in Dupont. Only a brief reference in the *Physiocratie* makes clear that he is here, as elsewhere, following Le Mercier.

C'est dans l'instant même où une erreur, certainement involontaire, puisqu'elle est contraire à son propre intérêt, arrache au Souverain une Ordonnance évidemment injuste, qu'un devoir impérieux vous prescrit de lui faire remarquer en quoi cette Ordonnance s'écarte des loix divines de l'ordre naturel, et l'impuissance où vous êtes de participer innocemment à son exécution.[32]

Thus the intervention of the judiciary should take place prior to any filing of suits by individual citizens damaged in their interests. The law might not be enforced and not impinge upon anybody's rights, but the violation of higher principles has to be corrected at once. In so doing, the court would not act in the capacity of an advisory body, but as a real constitutional court. Dupont is indeed anxious to warn that judges should never be allowed to take any part in drafting legislation.[33]

But Dupont, unlike Le Mercier, did not think of the Paris parliament as the most appropriate body to perform this task of revision. As a faithful follower of Turgot, he remembered the fight waged against his leader by Parliament during Turgot's tenure of office. Dupont did not trust a body "trop intrigant, trop jaloux d'une autorité usurpée, trop indifférent pour le véritable intérêt public, trop opposé à toute réforme de la législation, trop opiniâtre à conserver les formes dispendieuses de la procédure, trop vénal même vis-à-vis du gouvernement." [34] We may wonder whether it was this lack of faith in the oldest judiciary body of the kingdom and the inability to find any suitable and practicable substitute for it that caused Dupont to abandon the doctrine of judicial control he had so forcefully expounded, while still adhering to the doctrine of the limitation of legislative powers.

[32] *Physiocratie*, I, lxxxiv.
[33] *Ibid.*, I, lxxxvi.
[34] *Carl Friedrichs von Baden brieflicher Verkehr mit Mirabeau und Du Pont.* Letter of Dupont to Carl Ludwig von Baden (Paris, January 1, 1783), II, 352.

We do not know when the change took place. It was complete by 1789, as is revealed by the lengthy notes Dupont appended to a translation of Stevens' comparison of the British and the American constitution.[35]

The nineteenth note bears the title *Sur ce qu'il faut entendre par l'autorité législative, et jusqu'où on peut la déléguer.* The first point to be taken up is the extent of legislative power.

Il ne suffit pas qu'il soit vraisemblable que l'on n'abusera pas du pouvoir légis-latif; il faut qu'il soit impossible d'en abuser. Les nations et même les philosophes ont encore des idées très confuses sur *l'autorité législative.* L'autorité de faire toute espèce de loix, même celles qui seroient absurdes et injustes, ne peut être déléguée à personne; car elle n'appartient pas même au corps entier de la société. Si le corps entier de la société mû par des idées fanatiques, vouloit faire une loi contraire à la liberté, à la sûreté, au droit de propriété des citoyens, ou d'un seul citoyen, ordonner par exemple . . . qu'on jetteroit une partie des récoltes à la rivière sans indemniser les possesseurs; le citoyen isolé qui s'opposeroit à l'exécution d'une telle loi, pourroit être opprimé par la force supérieure des autres; il feroit vraisemblablement contre eux une guerre malheureuse, mais il ne seroit point *rebelle*, et en l'accablant de leur puissance, les autres citoyens, la société entière feroient un acte de tyrannie. Il faut donc poser en principe que *l'autorité législative* prise dans un sens étendu, qui em-brasseroit le pouvoir de tout faire ou de tout proscrire, est un droit que la nature s'est réservé, dont nulle association d'hommes ne peut s'emparer, qu'elle peut encore moins déléguer.[36]

At this point, however, we find that the vague words about the "essential law of nature," so dear to the physiocratic school, are translated into something more concrete. Just as Le Mercier was appealing in his later works to the "constitution," so Dupont is appealing now to a "declaration of rights": "*La législation* toute entière est renfermée dans une bonne *déclaration de droits.* La nation assemblée ne peut donner à personne l'autorité de faire des loix contraires à la déclaration des droits." But if all real legis-lative power is thus subtracted from the people's representatives, what scope is left to their actions?

Reste . . . *l'autorité* de faire *des réglemens* pour assûrer d'autant mieux la con-servation des droits: c'est cette *autorité* que, dans un sens restraint, l'on peut nommer *législative.* Le mot est parfaitement appliqué à la chose, et sembleroit indiquer que dans l'origine des sociétés les hommes ont eu des principes plus sûrs et des idées plus justes, que nous ne le croyons communément. Ils n'ont point dit *législateur* ce qui

[35] *Examen du gouvernement d'Angleterre comparé aux constitutions des Etats-Unis.* For a discussion of this translation, see below, p. 81.

[36] *Examen*, pp. 177–178. I am quoting at length these notes by Dupont to Stevens, because they have never been the subject of an accurate discussion and have never been reproduced verbatim. Schelle, the only one to mention them, gives a quotation which is not an exact reproduction of the original text (*Du Pont*, pp. 275–276).

auroit indiqué le pouvoir de *faire* arbitrairement des loix: ils ont dit, *législateur, porteur de loi.*[37]

Dupont has not, so far, contradicted his earlier stand, the essence of which was that the legislative bodies had only "declaratory," or, as he calls them now, "regulatory" powers. These regulatory acts have to stand a test of legitimacy now, as they did then. The touchstone is no longer natural law, but the declaration of rights:

Tout réglement a une pierre de touche: *Est-il conforme à la déclaration de droits, ou ne l'est-il pas?* Tout citoyen a le droit de lui faire subir l'essai de cette pierre de touche par une discussion libre, et communiquée aux autres citoyens avec toute l'étendue possible.[38]

But while in the *Physiocratie*, Dupont had insisted upon the judges' taking immediate cognizance of unlawful legislative acts so that the law of nature might at once be restored, in the *Examen* he is willing to admit a presumption of validity in every legislative enactment till the contrary has been proved.

Cette inaliénable liberté de discuter les *réglemens*, qu'on appelle improprement *loix*, et de les comparer avec *la déclaration de droits*, qui doit comprendre toutes les véritables loix de la société ne doit jamais emporter le droit de résister à ceux que la société a chargés et de rédiger, et de promulguer ces réglemens. L'exécution provisoire de ces ordres doit toujours être assûrée à l'autorité publique; et cela même est conforme à la loi fondamentale ou à la déclaration de droits, qui ne sauroit permettre que la volonté arbitraire, ou l'opinion d'un seul, ni de plusieurs individus, puisse porter atteinte à l'ordre général de la Société.[39]

In doubtful cases, however, this temporary enforcement is to be of the shortest possible duration:

Mais plus il est nécessaire que l'on obéisse avec une sévère exactitude aux *réglemens* ou à l'ordre provisoire, plus il importe, s'il est injuste, que cette obéissance ne soit pas prolongée au-delà de ce qui est indispensable pour le bon ordre, et que la déclaration de droits puisse reprendre aussi-tôt qu'il est possible toute son autorité, et que le réglement dérogatoire à cette déclaration puisse être promptement réformé.[40]

We are left to wonder who is going to "reform promptly" the regulatory act that runs against the declaration of rights. The first suggestion that it is no longer, in Dupont's mind, a judicial body is given by his assertion later on that there should be no bulwarks erected against the will of the people.

D'ailleurs, pourquoi vouloir élever des remparts contre ce qu'on appelle le pouvoir du peuple, ou plutôt de ses représentans? Il suffira que les représentans restent, comme ils doivent, sous la main de leurs commettans, pour ne jamais pouvoir former un corps ayant d'autres intérêts que le peuple.[41]

[37] *Examen*, pp. 178–179.
[38] *Ibid.*, pp. 179–180.
[39] *Ibid.*, p. 180.
[40] *Ibid.*, pp. 180–181.
[41] *Ibid.*, pp. 189–190.

Note twenty-one, entitled *Sur ce que le droit négatif ne peut pas être délégué, et sur les moyens naturels de prévenir tout abus de pouvoir législatif*, lets the cat out of the bag. Dupont is answering Stevens' statement that a dictatorial rule by the legislative body is inevitable, when no brakes on its activities are placed in the hands of the executive or judiciary powers. This is not true, according to Dupont, at least where the legislative power is (a) limited by a declaration of rights, (b) bound by fixed procedural and electoral rules, (c) answerable to county assemblies. In Dupont's words:

L'auteur revient encore ici à la nécessité prétendue de donner un droit négatif au pouvoir exécutif ou judiciaire, afin d'éviter l'abus du pouvoir législatif, confié à une seule chambre de représentans. Mais cet abus seroit-il à craindre; 1° Si cette chambre de représentans a son pouvoir limité par une déclaration des droits dont elle ne puisse changer aucun article? 2° Si elle ne peut, sous aucun prétexte, faire le moindre changement aux loix qui règlent sa propre constitution, la manière d'en élire les membres, la forme des délibérations, etc.? 3° Si les assemblées particulières des *comtés*, ont droit de se former pour les élections à des époques, fixes, et alors, si le corps législatif a changé quelque chose à sa constitution, ou violé la déclaration des droits, de charger ses nouveaux députés de révoquer ses actes contraires à la liberté; révocation contre laquelle le corps législatif ne pourroit revenir à moins que les comtés n'en eussent expressément chargé leurs députés? [42]

In the great struggle going on in these years on two continents it was clear that Dupont had thrown his lot with those who believed in an unimpeded popular legislative assembly, answerable to the people, it is true, and bound to those principles the people themselves had declared: no counterbalances, no insidious and hidden powers of control.[43] He had no objection to calling the three conditions he had laid down "un droit négatif."

Si on veut appeler ces moyens, ou d'autres qui leur ressembleroient, comme la nécessité du consentement d'assemblées formées dans les Comtés pour établir certaines loix, etc. Si, dis-je, on veut appeler ces moyens un droit négatif, j'y consens: mais alors on suivra l'ordre naturel; ce seront les citoyens eux-mêmes, ou du moins leurs représentans, plus immédiats, qui auront ce droit à l'égard du corps législatif. Une simple distinction bien faite entre les décisions prises à la pluralité des comtés exprimant chacun leur voeu; un réglement très-simple sur les pluralités nécessaires pour certaines décisions, sur la forme de ces décisions, réglemens que le simple bon sens peut inspirer; telles sont les véritables barrières qu'on doit opposer à un pouvoir législatif unique.[44]

[42] *Examen*, pp. 220–221.
[43] The somewhat different conclusions reached by Schelle (*Du Pont*, p. 276), are difficult to understand, especially when one considers that the general import of Dupont's notes was to answer Stevens' proposals for executive or judicial control of legislative actions.
[44] *Examen*, pp. 221–222.

There was thus nothing left of the doctrine of judicial control which seemed now to Dupont, on the eve of the French Revolution, to violate the equality of rights of the citizens. The only checks to be tolerated were those coming from the people brought together to elect new representatives and to chastise those who had betrayed their trust. Dupont did not ask himself how effectively and for how long the people would have been able to preserve intact the declaration of rights. To him, who hoped that the new order coming to birth in 1789 would bring about the realization of most of the "order" advocated by the physiocrats, and who had no longer to rely upon a waning royal power, this seemed to be the only way to follow. It was the only one that would have prevented the setting up of a "dangerous authority," [45] as he now called a supreme court passing judgment upon legislative acts, words very similar to those frequently used today in discussions of the same issue.

Dupont saw the coming and going of the revolution and took an active part in it. He saw the coming and going of the Napoleonic era and died an old man of seventy-eight in the free country where he had elected to spend the last years of his life, America. His literary labours during these long years were remarkable.[46] He was an active speaker at the Constituent Assembly and at the *Conseil des anciens*, writing also extensive reports. He directed the *Correspondance patriotique* and *L'Historien*, being one of their most frequent contributors and their strictest constitutionalist. Hiding in 1793 from the hand of the Terror, he wrote a *Philosophie de l'univers*, where Hobbes is called "insensé" and Rousseau "cet éloquent menteur qui, cependant, aimait la vérité." [47] He advised the United States on the best system of national education, edited the works of Turgot, submitted to the Institut a number of papers on natural science topics, and addressed to J. B. Say a vehement defense of the work of the physiocratic school.

Yet we find little that is new. It is natural that his ideas on government should have become fixed. His individualism remained tempered by a consciousness of the individual's duty to the state, and he worked hard to keep alive the belief in the necessity of the rule of law. That he had reason, as Schelle suggests,[48] to lament his

---

[45] *Examen*, p. 222.

[46] For a very accurate and complete bibliography of Dupont, see Schelle, *Du Pont*, pp. 399–432.

[47] *Philosophie de l'univers* (Paris, 1796), p. 61.   [48] Schelle, *Du Pont*, p. 292.

earlier participation in the diffusion of the doctrine of legal despotism, seeing the dreadful use to which it could be turned in revolutionary times, we may doubt, because that doctrine was not at all
despotic. Dupont hated despots all his life. The only real shift
had taken place in his conception of the relative weight to be given
the legislative power within the frame of government. He continued to be willing to grant it a greater independence from outward control than before, even though still limiting its capacity of
action. His dislike of the then abolished parliament of Paris as a
final court of review had not disappeared. Writing, as a member
from Nemours of the Constituent Assembly, on the frequency of
national assemblies, he makes clear what is to be the legislative
process. The upper chamber could have the right to reject three
times any proposal (*arrêté*) coming from the lower house. When
finally approved by both houses, the *arrêté* becomes a *décret*. The
royal sanction is then necessary to transform it into a *loi*. This
power of sanction belonged prior to 1789 to the parliament.

Tel étoit le droit que les Parlemens opposoient au Roi, par les remontrances, par les
refus d'enregistrement, dans le temps, heureusement loin de nous, quoiqu'il ne soit
passé que depuis quelques mois, où nos Rois exerçoient les fonctions du Peuple, et
où les Parlemens s'étoient emparés de celles du Prince.[49]

What would happen, should the king refuse his sanction to a
décret? The issue should be brought before the people

> XI. Si le roi refuse sa sanction à un décret de l'assemblée nationale, les lettres de
> convocation pour l'année suivante inviteront les Electeurs à donner la plus
> sérieuse attention à la proposition qui auroit été faite et rejetée; et les Elec-
> teurs exprimeront leur voeu sur cette question par l'affirmation, par la néga-
> tion ou par le silence.
> XII. Si la pluralité des électeurs n'exprime pas un voeu affirmatif, le projet de loi
> qui auroit été rejeté par le Roi, ne pourra être proposé de nouveau l'année
> suivante.
> XIII. Si la pluralité des électeurs regarde le projet de loi comme utile, la Chambre
> des Représentans en renouvellera la proposition; et si après qu'elle aura
> subi toutes les formalités nécessaires à un décret de l'Assemblée Nationale,
> elle devient en effet le voeu de l'Assemblée, le Roi ne pourra y refuser sa
> sanction.[50]

Having survived the Terror, Dupont took an active part in the
discussion of the new constitution of 1795. He was afraid of a
weak and divided executive power in the hands of a directory

[49] *De la périodicité des Assemblées Nationales*, p. 19.
[50] *Projet d'articles relatifs à la constitution de l'Assemblée Nationale*. The project
is in 13 articles.

lacking any unity of policies and of a legislative body "toujours assemblé, toujours délibérant, n'annonçant point de vacances, voulant sans cesse faire et défaire les loix." Once the five fundamental codes were approved, the legislative power would have been freed of its main burden, and no more than three or four laws each year would be needed.[51] His anxiety was not lessened by the publication of the project of the Committee of Eleven, which betrayed the republican principles of '89 and was unfair to the peasants whose electoral rights were restricted.[52] He repeated to the end his interpretation of the true significance of the word *legislator*. An injust ordinance "ne sauroit être obligatoire pour la conscience," [53] he wrote to Jefferson in 1811, showing himself, incidentally, totally unaware of the constitutional developments that had taken place in the United States in the years following the adoption of the Constitution. No other remedy is offered against such injust ordinances except a *suspensive veto* by the executive power.[54] The position taken twenty-three years before had not been reversed, and the doctrine of judicial control had never been invoked again.

[51] *Constitution pour la République française*, p. 104.
[52] *Observations sur la constitution*, p. 5.
[53] *The Correspondence of Jefferson and Du Pont de Nemours.* Letter of December 12, 1811, p. 177.
[54] Letter of Dupont to Jefferson, Paris, April 14, 1812, *Correspondence*, pp. 195–196.

CHAPTER VII

THE RECEPTION IN FRANCE OF THE PHYSIOCRATIC DOCTRINE OF JUDICIAL CONTROL

1. THE SCHOOL AND THE DOCTRINE

THIS review of physiocratic thought with regard to the problem of judicial control has revealed many vivid contrasts and considerable variety in the approach to the common center of interest of the school, the preservation of a social order where light had superseded darkness. Quesnay limited himself to a generic discussion, repeatedly pointing, however, to the supremacy which the courts enjoyed in the ideal state, China. And although Mirabeau did not provide any specific remedy against the deterioration of the machine of government, merely stressing the catastrophic consequences which would befall it in case the rules of the natural order failed of application, in at least one instance he let it be implicitly understood that he favored a measure of control vested in judicial bodies.

It is with Le Mercier that the doctrine takes its definite shape and receives its most complete treatment. Not only did Le Mercier give it a clear-cut expression; he translated what at first had been a theory based purely upon a rational appeal to natural law into a doctrine placed at the core of a constitutional system. We must recognize in him a coherence and persistence which Dupont, for all the great qualities of his writings, did not have. Dupont expounded the doctrine of judicial control with the fervor of a youthful convert and did more to foster its acceptance by the rank and file of the school than any other; but, as we have seen, he relinquished his earlier stand and favored, within the limits of the Bill of Rights, an unimpeded legislative power, with no judiciary authority empowered to say when those limits had been trespassed upon. Times had changed, and other methods looked more promising for the attainment of his program. This new attitude, however, came late and did not threaten the unity of the school in its period of greatest development, the late sixties. Against the attacks of Mably, La Vauguyon wrote a very brilliant as well as persuasive paper, in which the defense of judicial review was made one of its important points. Butré did the same, maintaining his favorable attitude toward judicial control in later writings. And everywhere in Le Trosne's work is felt the awe-inspiring superiority of constitutional laws and the necessity of judges bound to support them.

Thus, acceptance of the doctrine of judicial review by the physiocratic school is not alone to be found in isolated instances, but can be said to represent the common opinion of nearly all its important members. This is confirmed by a reading of the sixty-three volumes of their principal journal, the *Ephémérides du citoyen*, a periodical whose perusal affords much enlightenment on the activities of the school. We see, for instance, the anonymous and still unidentified reviewer of Martin Hübner's "Essai sur l'histoire du droit naturel" in the first volume of the journal qualify as "holy" the author's assertion that positive laws were to be strictly derived from natural laws,[1] yet grow indignant over the fact that the same Hübner, having dedicated 273 pages "à détailler l'Histoire des Loix naturelles chez les Romains, peuple *féroce, ignorant, brigand et destructeur*, qui n'eut jamais, à proprement parler, ni *Loix*, ni *Gouvernement*," got rid of the Chinese in nine pages.[2]

The publication of Le Mercier's *Ordre* excited numerous comments, favorable and unfavorable alike, being, as it was, the first complete statement of physiocratic doctrine.[3] An unknown follower wrote a *précis* of the book. He brought into relief what Le Mercier had said about the duties of the magistrates, making his own Le Mercier's theory in the following words:

Magistrats, pour décider dans les cas particuliers quelle doit être l'application des loix de l'ordre naturel, réduites en loix positives par l'autorité souveraine; et qui ont le devoir impérieux de comparer les Ordonnances des Souverains avec les Loix

[1] *Ephémérides* (1767), I, 103. Hübner had written about the great variety of positive laws: "Cependant toutes ces loix, quelque différentes qu'elles soient entre elles, se ressemblent et doivent se ressembler en ce qu'elles ne sont qu'une explication ou extension du Droit Naturel. Elles ne doivent donc jamais rien contenir qui soit contraire à ces loix primitives, sur lesquelles la Puissance législative même de leurs Auteurs est fondée" (*Essai sur l'histoire du droit naturel* [London, 1757–58, 2 volumes], I, 3).

[2] *Ephémérides*, p. 107. The Chinese, of course, were considered by the physiocrats as a happy people who had established an ideal form of government, and one of Quesnay's important essays had been on Chinese despotism. See above, pp. 30–31.

[3] For Mably's *Doutes*, see below, pp. 69–71; for La Vauguyon's answer see above, pp. 38–40.

de la Justice par essence, avant de s'engager à prendre ces Ordonnances positives pour règle de leur jugemens.[4]

That this interpretation of the judges' duties was the interpretation of the school as such came to be generally accepted at the time. It was not open to question that in the physiocratic state the same judges "chargés de faire l'application des diverses loix positives aux cas particuliers, ont le devoir, le droit, et de plus un intérêt très pressant d'avertir le Souverain de son erreur toutes les fois qu'il pourroit lui échapper une ordonnance opposée à la conservation des droits de la nation." [5] These words, coming as they do from the pen of a public functionary, are very cautious and do not admit the whole of the physiocratic doctrine, which went far beyond the mere granting of an advisory capacity to the judges. But they are revealing and give an indication of the misgivings entertained in governmental circles concerning the possible consequences of a doctrine that undermined royal power. In 1770, when the government began to frown upon physiocratic activities, we witness the amusing effort of the censor of the *Ephémérides*, Moreau, to reconcile the belief that a positive law running against a law of nature is not binding and should be voided, with the sternly realistic view of the times that all laws should always be obeyed.

Tel est l'empire absolu de la raison et de la justice que les ordres qui contreviennent directement à ce qu'elles prescrivent, ne se produisent jamais sous la forme d'une loi générale. Il n'y a jamais eu de Gouvernement qui ait prescrit l'homicide, aucune magistrature qui ait entrepris de changer les tems des labours et des récoltes; supposer de telles loix possibles, c'est admettre que la société peut obéir à des ordres imbéciles.[6]

Notwithstanding this remarkable development, the doctrine failed to produce any permanent impression on the constitutional life of France for reasons which have already been analyzed in part, and upon which we shall touch again in our concluding pages. We must now consider the criticisms with which the doctrine was met.

[4] *Ephémérides* (1767), XII, 187.
[5] "Lettre de Monsieur M., censeur royal, à un magistrat," *Ephémérides* (1768), IX, 147. This letter was prompted by the publication of the *Précis de l'ordre légal* by Mirabeau, who, however, had contributed nothing positive to the doctrine of judicial review.
[6] "Corps de doctrine du censeur actuel des Ephémérides du citoyen," *Ephémérides* (1770), I, 268–269.

2. THE CONTEMPORARY CRITICS

It is no wonder that the physiocratic doctrine did not go unchallenged in its own time. In that "age of paper" the contrary would have been remarkable, and a proof of meager intellectual interest in it. As is well known, the entire political and economic doctrine of the school gave origin to a bitter debate, in which practically every important literary figure of the period took part — Voltaire in the lead with his famous *Homme aux quarante écus*.

At first the criticisms dealt mainly with the economic aspects of the teachings of the physiocrats,[7] the weightiest attack against which was delivered by Forbonnais in his *Principes et observations économiques*.[8] But the extension of the doctrine to the political field, and especially the publication of Le Mercier's *Ordre naturel* in 1767, quickly drew fire from a number of redoubtable writers, who, above all, objected to the introduction of the concept of legal despotism. The most brilliant as well as the most damaging attack came from Mably's *Doutes proposés aux philosophes économistes sur l'ordre naturel et essentiel des sociétés politiques*.[9]

He was also the first, and we may say the only one, to criticize with any detail and comprehensiveness the doctrine of judicial control of legislative acts. Mably had witnessed the futile resistance which the Paris parliament had put up against the king and therefore was anxious to have the physiocrats explain what new powers they had given to their magistrates for the performance of their duty and what guarantees existed against possible betrayal of the great hopes the people would place in the judiciary: "Si, dans un pays où l'évidence est connue, la puissance législative peut être surprise, pourquoi les magistrats ne le seront-ils jamais? Si le despote peut trahir ses devoirs ou ses intérêts, pourquoi les magistrats seront-ils fidellement attachés aux leurs?"[10]

Le Mercier's assumption that the magistrates could not err because the "evidence" of the natural order would assist them,

---

[7] For a brief, but complete, summary of the writings of about a score of opponents of the school, cf. Higgs, *The Physiocrats*, pp. 102 ff. Higgs does not mention Béardé de l'Abbaye and Le Gros.

[8] Amsterdam, 1767, 2 volumes.

[9] First edition, Paris, 1768. We quote from *Collection complète des Oeuvres* (Paris, 1794–95), vol. XI.

[10] *Doutes*, pp. 59–60.

was, according to Mably, rather weak. The same possibility of error existed for the magistrates and for the legislative power. Were it not so, and were the magistrates free from committing those mistakes in which the legislative power persisted, then Mably would ask the physiocrats:

> Pour quelle raison vous ne placez pas plutôt la puissance législative dans ce corps infaillible que dans un despote que vous avouez être capable de se laisser surprendre par ses passions ou par celles de ses ministres. Il auroit été plus court de donner l'infaillibilité à votre despote; mais alors des magistrats gardiens, dépositaires et défenseurs des loix, auroient été hors d'oeuvre dans votre politique.[11]

According to Mably, the strength of the "evidence" was purely imaginary, since ignorance was the natural condition of men, and fortune, passion, and accident could alter or destroy the best calculated rational plans. "Puisque notre auteur en revient à la force de son évidence, j'en reviens, de mon côté, à la force de mes passions," [12] Mably says, appealing to what he considers the true ruling forces of mankind.

But Le Mercier's system was not only weak in its premises; it was also contradictory in its plan, as when, for instance, Le Mercier set up again as guardian of the law the sovereign (and legislative) power, forgetting what he had previously said about the magistrates.

> C'étoit bien la peine [exclaims the disillusioned Mably], de créer tant de tribunaux et de magistrats . . . il est question de trouver un gardien, un dépositaire, un protecteur des loix contre les entreprises, la foiblesse ou la bonne volonté d'un despote qu'on reconnoît sujet á l'erreur, et après de longs circuits, on revient à me dire que c'est ce despote lui-même qui doit garder, défendre et protéger les loix. [13]

The truth is, says Mably, that not in the despotic system of government set up by the physiocrats (no less despotic because judicial control had been added to it) is to be found the safeguard of the principles of natural law, but in a system of checks and balances: "Alors tous les ordres de la société se balancent, s'imposent, se tiennent en équilibre; . . . et c'est alors que la nation . . . est véritablement la dépositaire et la protectrice de ses loix."[14]

---

[11] *Doutes*, p. 60.

[12] *Ibid.*, p. 230.

[13] *Ibid.*, p. 66. What Le Mercier had said was that to the sovereign pertained a procedural control upon the magistrate's actions, "sans entrer dans l'examen du fonds" (cf. *L'Ordre*, chap. XXV). This left the substance of his theory of judicial control intact and was something very different from what Mably made it out to be.

[14] *Doutes*, p. 71.

Mably justifies this system on the basis of history and the necessity of preventing too sudden changes in the government of society,[15] increasing the historical flavor of his reasoning by an appeal to the experience of the past and by exclaiming: "Que la métaphysique est quelquefois déplacée dans les choses morales!" [16]

Only one other contemporary writer followed Mably in discussing the doctrine of judicial review, Béardé de l'Abbaye.[17] The doctrine of legal despotism seems vicious to him, despite all the efforts of Dupont to clip the wings of the legislative power, which is thus no longer a legislative power at all.

M. Dup. croit sauver la difficulté en disant *que le pouvoir législatif, qui ne peut pas être celui de créer, mais seulement de déclarer les loix, d'en assurer l'observance, appartient exclusivement au Souverain.* Tout cela veut dire que les législateurs ne sont pas législateurs. Mais si le Souverain ne fait que déclarer les loix, il les sait donc déjà, et dans le cas qu'elles existassent de même dans l'âme de tous les hommes, avant sa déclaration, sans lui elles seroient connues de tous les hommes, ainsi sa déclaration seroit très inutile. C'est donc le prétendu juste absolu qui sera le véritable législateur, mais ce juste absolu ayant été ignoré de tous les peuples, comme le dit M. Merc., où l'ira-t-on chercher? [18]

Under the physiocratic system, adds Béardé de l'Abbaye, one has to look elsewhere for a true expression of legislative power. One has to look to the courts, which have been made all-powerful and, vested with functions of control, have been set up as the real legislative bodies.

Les magistrats, dit M. Dup., *sont réligieusement obligés de commencer par juger les loix positives.* Voici des magistrats bien plus puissans que leur Souverain, qui n'a que le droit de déclarer les loix, tandis qu'ils ont celui de juger. Or, juger les loix, c'est ou les condamner, ou les approuver, c'est, ou les rejetter, et pour lors elles ne sont plus rien, ou les admettre, et ce n'est que dès ce moment qu'elles deviennent loix. Ce sont donc les magistrats, qui donnent la sanction aux loix, ce sont donc les magistrats, qui sont législateurs.[19]

[15] *Ibid.*, p. 240.

[16] *Ibid.*, p. 238.

[17] *Recherches sur les moyens de supprimer les impôts, précédées de l'examen de la nouvelle science* (Amsterdam, 1770).

[18] *Recherches*, pp. 147–148.

[19] *Ibid.*, p. 148. Baudeau answered this attack in the *Ephémérides du citoyen* (1770), VII, 77–137. He had been the founder of the *Ephémérides* and had turned it over to the school in a moment when every other avenue of public expression was closed. He was thus an important member of the school. Not for this reason alone. His *Exposition de la loi naturelle* (Paris, 1767) had been one of the early important theoretical expressions of physiocratic doctrine. Those property rights which, as conceived by the physiocrats, attracted so many criticisms, were to him the cornerstone of every society: *"Sûreté des propriétés:* voilà tout le pacte social en trois mots: l'abrégé de toutes les *loix naturelles*, et le germe unique des vraies *loix*

Béardé had raised one of the burning issues in the debate on judicial control. It unfortunately entirely escaped the attention of Linguet. In 1770, when Dupont wrote a review of Linguet's *Théorie des loix*,[20] he did not bring into the discussion the problem of the ultimate control of legislative acts. Thus, when the sharp-tongued Linguet undertook to answer Dupont,[21] he was satisfied to stress the bad faith, buffoonery, and indecency of the several abbots, watchmakers, and provincial judges composing the physiocratic sect,[22] without discussing at all the validity of the doctrine of judicial control.

That issue was already beginning to recede into the background. From then on, other features of the physiocratic system captured the limelight.

---

positives" (*Exposition*, p. 27). Positive laws were but the application and translation of natural laws (p. 52), something which the human legislator should never forget. Happiness and peace were certain to come from the unchallenged rule of the "order" (p. 70). In 1777 Baudeau had to answer Graslin on a strictly economic point: cf. *Correspondence entre M. Graslin . . . et M. l'Abbé Baudeau . . . , sur un des principes fondamentaux de la doctrine des soi-disants Philosophes Economistes*, (Londres, Paris, 1777).

[20] *Ephémérides du citoyen* (1770), VI, 161–248.

[21] Cf. *Réponse aux docteurs modernes* (Paris, 1771), 2 volumes.

[22] *Ibid.*, I, 7–9.

CHAPTER VIII

PHYSIOCRACY AND AMERICA

1. INDEPENDENCE AND THE CONSTITUTION

As early as 1750 Turgot, then a young man of twenty-three, in a speech at the Sorbonne, was prophesying American independence. One day America would be free, since historical experience had taught the lesson that colonies, like fruits, "ne tiennent à l'arbre que jusqu'à leur maturité." [1] From that moment on, the issue of American independence was ever present to the physiocratic school, which, besides showing the greatest sympathy towards the efforts of the colonists, entertained the hope that the thirteen colonies might prove an immensely valuable testing ground of the economic and political doctrines of physiocracy, to the future advantage of all mankind.

First, however, freedom had to be won. The constitutional settlement of the country would come once that freedom had been achieved. For this reason the physiocrats were anxious to put the American case before their country, and when Franklin gave his famous testimony before the House of Commons on the occasion of the repeal of the Stamp Act, a complete translation of it appeared in the *Ephémérides du citoyen*.[2] To Dupont the righteousness of the American cause was never in doubt. He held in great admiration the hardy people beyond the ocean, leading such a simple and brotherly life near to the land, that greatest of all sources of wisdom and strength. "Et c'est ce peuple que des marchands exclusifs veulent opprimer. Vous n'êtes pas surpris sans doutes, Monsieur, de qu'ils commencent à y trouver de la difficulté." [3] The future of the colonies was assured: "Il ne leur faut pas un siècle et demi pour former un empire plus puissant que ce n'est aujourd'hui l'Europe entière." [4] Turgot, on the other

---

[1] "Sur les progrès successifs de l'esprit humain," Dec. 11, 1750, *Oeuvres* (Paris, 1808–11, ed. Dupont), II, 66.

[2] "Des troubles qui divisent l'Angleterre et ses colonies," *Ephémérides* (1768), VII, 28–41; VIII, 159–192.

[3] "Lettre de M. H. [Dupont] à l'auteur des Ephémérides, au sujet du Pays florissant qui n'a point de villes," *Ephémérides* (1769), VIII, 49.

[4] *Ibid.*

hand, in an interesting memorandum submitted to the king in
1776, although reasserting his early view that American independence was inevitable, did not hesitate to conclude that in the
interest of the crown the best thing would be an English victory
over the colonies. This would relieve any subsequent pressure
otherwise certain to be felt upon the French colonies.[5] From a
different point of view, the Abbé Roubaud also joined the political
realists in stressing the great significance of the altered balance
of power on the American continent that had followed the Treaty
of Paris of 1763:

> La guerre actuelle de la Grande-Bretagne avec l'Amérique septentrionale est
> l'effet de celle-ci [the British conquest of Canada] et de ses succès. Ces succès ont
> delivré les colonies angloises d'un voisin redoutable, et la protection de la metropole
> leur est devenue inutile et pesante.[6]

Such subtle political calculations, however, did not dim the
enthusiasm of Le Trosne for the endurance, the wisdom, and the
prudence of the American people fighting for the preservation
of rights that had been historically theirs:

> Ce sont des hommes libres, pleins de prudence, de sagesse et de modération, qui
> connoissent, par sentiment et par expérience, les droits et les devoirs de l'homme
> et du Citoyen, les bornes nullement arbitraires du commandement et de l'obéissance,
> les véritables rapports de la société, et les obligations de la confédération civile; qui
> après avoir, par des travaux infatigables, changé des déserts en un territoire fertile,
> ne réclament que l'exercice des droits de la propriété et de la liberté des échanges;
> qui offensés par une longue suite de mauvais traitemens, ont sçu souffrir tant qu'ils
> ont eu l'espérance d'obtenir le redressement de leurs griefs; qui ont mis dans leurs
> représentations, depuis la naissance des troubles, un ton de sagesse, une force de
> raisonnement, une éloquence noble, aussi admirable que leur conduite et leurs
> démarches; qui attachés à la mere Patrie par les liens respectables de l'association
> civile, qu'on ne doit jamais rompre qu'à la derniere extrémité, et plus encore par
> ceux de la reconnoissance, se sont montrés plus sensibles qu'elle à la rupture, ont
> mis tout en oeuvre pour l'éviter, ou du moins pour reculer, autant qu'il auroit été
> possible, le moment de la scission, que la vue et les principes oppresseurs de la
> Métropole leur faisaient envisager, comme étant tôt ou tard inévitable.[7]

Le Trosne believed that a magnificent future was in store for
the United States, ruled by the "laws of the social order," faithful to the "laws of nature," and a haven of refuge, "où les hommes
de toutes les contrées, chassés par la misère, par les entraves sans

---

[5] "Mémoire sur la manière dont la France et l'Espagne devoient envisager les
suites de la querelle entre la Grande-Bretagne et ses colonies," *Oeuvres*, VIII, 495.

[6] "Réflexions politiques sur l'Amérique," *Nouvelles Éphémérides économiques*
(1776), III, 61.

[7] *Réflexions politiques sur la guerre actuelle de l'Angleterre avec ses colonies, et
sur l'état de la Russie* (January 1777), p. 2.

nombre mises aux travaux et à l'industrie, par l'intolérance . . .
trouveront un asyle toujours ouvert." [8] But he warned the Americans to settle the problem of taxation in their fundamental law if
they wished to avoid the corruption, the unending troubles, and
the political oppression which on that score had beset the European
countries.

This was the first advice given America by the physiocrats on
the constitutional issue that was to open an ever widening gulf
between the doctrines of the physiocrats and those of such leaders
of American thought as Adams and Jefferson. At first, however,
the contrast that was to develop later was not apparent, and
harmony between the French school and the American political
revolutionists seemed to exist, fostered by the benevolent utterances of Benjamin Franklin, then the best-known interpreter in
Europe of the ideals of his country, and said by Dupont to have
become "un des plus habiles adeptes de cette science sublime" [9]
which was the doctrine of Quesnay.

Thus, in the years immediately following the publication of
L'Ordre naturel et essentiel des sociétés politiques and of the
Origine et progrès d'une science nouvelle, with the school unanimous in support of the theory entrusting the magistrates with the
defense and safeguard of fundamental laws, we find in the *Ephémérides du citoyen* a sympathetic echo of the similar doctrine
then being discussed, with increasingly widespread approval, in the
thirteen colonies. Of all the American writings dedicated to an
analysis of the future constitutional settlement of the country, the
privilege of being translated and reproduced in full in the pages
of the school's periodical went to the two letters which Abraham
Mansword had published in the *Pennsylvania Chronicle*.[10] The

---

[8] *Ibid.*, pp. 8–9.

[9] *Ephémérides* (1768), VII, 32–33.

[10] "Lettres d'Abraham Mansword, Citoyen de Philadelphie, à ses compatriotes
de l'Amérique septentrionale; traduites du Pennsylvany's Chronicle," *Ephémérides*
(1771), X, 75–112; XI, 6–45. The letters are dated from Philadelphia April 12
and May 15, 1771, and are preceded by an *Avertissement* in which we read, among
other things, that "on se livre beaucoup à l'instruction dans cet heureux pays, et
c'est d'elle qu'on attend la prospérité générale. Nous tenons du célèbre Franklin
qu'il n'y a point d'artisan en Pensylvanie qui, en déjeûnant, ne lise les papiers publics, et, pendant une heure après son dîner, quelques bons ouvrages de philosophie
ou de politique." I have been unable to consult the files of the *Pennsylvania Chronicle*. As far as I could ascertain, the only reference in American literature to the
author's name is contained in a letter addressed to Dupont by Franklin: "Abraham
Mansword's Advice to his countrymen is very good. I hope they will have more

reason was Mansword's belief that the fundamental law should embody the three great principles of property, freedom, and security and that the magistrates should be appointed to see that these principles were respected. These were also the doctrines of the physiocratic school, and Dupont and his friends were always very eager for direct or indirect approval from foreign countries. Mansword seems to envisage a constituent assembly, meeting at regular intervals and recognized as the supreme authority of the land when in session. During the intervals it was necessary to have a supreme court with the duty of preserving the fundamental laws in all their integrity.

> . . . dans l'intervalle d'une assemblée à l'autre, il est vraisemblable que le corps politique sera représenté par un conseil présidé par un chef, pour toutes les affaires de l'administration civile et économique de notre république. Il sera représenté pareillement par un corps de magistrature supérieure, pour tout ce qui regardera l'administration de la justice, et la conservation de nos loix fondamentales dans toute leur intégrité. . . . Il doit donc toujours exister dans notre République un Corps de Magistrature, un Corps dépositaire des loix, chargé seul et exclusivement de faire parler les loix, de faire agir l'autorité des loix, de prononcer et de faire exécuter les jugemens rendus d'avance par les loix; et ce Corps doit être institué de maniere qu'il ne puisse jamais cesser d'être véritablement le Ministre de la justice, véritablement l'organe des loix.[11]

Only God was the true legislator.[12]

This harmony was not going to last the moment the democratic trend of the American Revolution became apparent. An indication of the inevitable break is to be gathered from Mirabeau's unpublished "Observations sur la déclaration des droits du bon peuple de Virginie, portée le 1er juin 1776." [13] The Declaration "con-

---

of it" (London, June 15, 1772, *The Writings of B. Franklin*, ed. A. H. Smyth [New York, 1905–07], V, 105–106). The *Dictionary of American Biography* does not mention Mansword's name.

[11] First letter, pp. 96 and 108.

[12] Second letter, p. 24.

[13] Archives Nationales de Paris, M. 784, n. 37 (1–3). There is no printed edition of the "Observations." A few excerpts have been given by Weulersse in *Les Manuscripts économiques de Quesnay et de Mirabeau*, pp. 143–146. Weulersse describes the manuscript as being fragmentary (pp. 7, 9 and 146). Upon careful study of the manuscript as it exists today in the Archives, obviously after the "désordre," of which Weulersse complains, has been remedied, I believe it to be complete. The three bundles are not all in Mirabeau's handwriting. There is some duplication, but no part is missing, as it is easy to see since Mirabeau comments upon each article of the Declaration in consecutive order. The number of articles upon which Mirabeau comments is eighteen, while the number of articles in all American texts of the Declaration is sixteen. Since Mirabeau accompanies his "Observations" with a French text of the Declaration, it could easily be established that he used

serve quelques principes que je croirois être dangereux et exagérés dans leurs conséquences s'ils étaient posés comme base universelle des constitutions sociales." The principle he finds affirmed in the first article, that all men are born equally free and independent, arouses misgivings in him, for it fails to stress the idea of duty, to Mirabeau of even greater value: "Regardez cette pauvre créature qui vient de naître, et appliquez lui les pompeuses paroles . . . qui dit libre, dit franc et quitte, à ce qu'il me semble. Or, il faut avoir mis à côté et parfaitement oublié les devoirs." Similarly, the doctrine that all authority belongs to the people has never been a part of the tenets of the physiocrats. Rather, they have stressed the great importance of public opinion and the obedience due the law of nature. "Ils ont dit seulement que l'opinion était au fond la puissance dominante entre les hommes; que la domination de chacune d'elles était solide et durable en proportion de ce qu'elle s'accordait avec les lumières de la raison."

Both equality and popular sovereignty were assailed. Mirabeau's attack, however, remained unknown, while another controversy of greater importance had been publicly under way for several years. Turgot had started it with his letter [14] to Price of March 12, 1778.

It is true that in his letter Turgot calls America the hope of mankind, but his eulogy is tinged with apprehension.

Il est impossible de ne pas faire des voeux pour que ce peuple parvienne à toute la prospérité dont il est susceptible. Il est l'espérance du genre-humain. Il peut en devenir le modèle. Il doit prouver au monde, par le fait, que les hommes peuvent être libres et tranquilles, et peuvent se passer des chaînes de toute espèce que les tyrans et les charlatans de toute robe ont prétendu leur imposer sous le prétexte du bien public. Il doit donner l'exemple de la liberté politique, de la liberté religieuse, de la liberté du commerce et de l'industrie. L'asyle qu'il ouvre à tous les opprimés

the French translation as given in Filippo Mazzei, *Recherches historiques et politiques sur les Etats-Unis* (Paris, 1788), I, 158–163. Mazzei, probably basing his work upon some preliminary draft (which is not given, however, in the *Proceedings of the Convention of May 1776* (ed. 1816)), divided article VI into two, and added a new one (article IX in Mazzei), running as follows: "Toutes les loix rétroactives, et punissant les délits commis avant qu'elles existassent, sont injustes, et par conséquent ne doivent jamais avoir lieu." The writing of the "Observations" can thus be definitely assigned to some time between the publication of Mazzei's *Recherches* in April 1788 (cf. *Correspondence par Grimm et Diderot* [Paris, 1877–78, ed. Maurice Tourneux], XV, 251), and Mirabeau's death on July 13, 1789. On the Virginia Declaration, cf. also Mirabeau's letter to his brother, Argenteuil, April 26, 1788, "Lettres inédites du Marquis de Mirabeau," ed. Meunier, *Le Correspondant* (Paris, Feb. 25, 1913), pp. 697–698.

[14] *Oeuvres*, IX, 376–392.

de toutes les Nations, doit consoler la terre. La facilité d'en profiter pour se dérober aux suites d'un mauvais Gouvernement, forcera les Gouvernemens Européens d'être justes et de s'éclairer; le reste du monde ouvrira peu à peu les yeux sur le néant de l'illusion dont les politiques se sont bercés. Mais il faut pour cela que l'Amérique s'en garantisse, et qu'elle ne redevienne pas, comme l'ont tant répété vos écrivains ministériels, une image de notre Europe, un amas de Puissances divisées, se disputant des territoires ou des profits de commerce, et cimentant continuellement l'esclavage des peuples par leur propre sang.[15]

The last sentence strikingly indicates what Turgot believed to be the main issue at stake: the power of the central government versus the power of the several states. But if this problem was Turgot's chief concern, many were the doubts entertained by him of the wisdom of the path pursued until then by the constitution-makers of the different states. Price had criticized Pennsylvania for exacting a religious oath from members of the House of Representatives; but Turgot points to even worse oaths imposed by other states. In addition, no state had paid any attention "à la grande distinction, la seule fondée sur la nature, entre deux classes d'hommes, celle des propriétaires de terres, et celle des non-propriétaires; à leurs intérêts et par conséquent à leurs droits différens relativement à la législation." [16]

Still, he was anxious to prove that the two chief mistakes committed were, on the one hand, the lack of any provision for a centralized government which should give real unity to the dis-membered forces of the single states; on the other, the absence of the needed concentration of powers within each state. According to him, this tendency to be found in the rising constitutional structures of all American states represented a complete denial of the very core of the physiocratic doctrine, namely, centralization of all functions of the state in the hands of the sovereign.

It may be pointed out here that Turgot's interpretation of the nature of the physiocratic state omits that most important element which had been used by the more representative and orthodox members of the school to reëstablish an otherwise badly upset equilibrium: judicial control. The control of magistrates was a limitation upon the sovereign power which Turgot had never accepted.

He was following, however, the school's tradition in decrying the system of checks and balances, which he believed to be but a humble imitation of the English system:

[15] *Oeuvres*, IX, 388–389.   [16] *Ibid.*, 382.

Je vois dans le plus grand nombre [of constitutions] l'imitation sans objet des usages de l'Angleterre. Au lieu de ramener toutes les autorités à une seule, celle de la nation, l'on établit des corps différens, un corps de représentans, un conseil, un gouverneur, parce que l'Angleterre a une Chambre des Communes, une Chambre Haute et un Roi. On s'occupe à balancer ces différens pouvoirs: comme si cet équilibre de forces, qu'on a pu croire nécessaire pour balancer l'énorme prépondérance de la royauté, pouvoit être de quelque usage dans des républiques fondées sur l'égalité de tous les citoyens; et comme si tout ce qui établit différens corps, n'étoit pas une source de divisions.[17]

A multiplication and improper distribution of the functions of government had proceeded alongside the multiplication of its organs.

Je ne vois pas qu'on se soit assez occupé de réduire au plus petit nombre possible les genres d'affaires dont le gouvernement de chaque état sera chargé; ni à séparer les objets de législation de ceux d'administration générale, et de ceux d'administration particulière et locale; à constituer des assemblées locales subalternes qui remplissant presque toutes les fonctions de détail du Gouvernement dispensent les assemblées générales de s'en occuper, et ôtent aux membres de celles-ci tout moyen et peut-être tout désire d'abuser d'une autorité qui ne peut s'appliquer qu'à des objets généraux, et par là même étrangers aux petites passions qui agitent les hommes.[18]

And, what was particularly offensive to the physiocratic mind, free trade was far from being an accepted fact.

On suppose partout le droit de régler le commerce; on autorise même les corps exclusifs, ou les gouverneurs, à prohiber l'exportation de certaines denrées dans certaines occurrences; tant on est loin d'avoir senti que la loi de la liberté entière de tout commerce est un corollaire du droit de propriété; tant on est encore plongés dans les brouillards des illusions européennes.[19]

Paralleling in a larger and higher sphere this lack of unity and of administrative organization in the various states was the weak nature of the bond which tied together the several parts.

Dans l'union générale des provinces entre elles, je ne vois pas une coalition, une fusion de toutes les parties, qui n'en fasse qu'un corps un et homogène. Ce n'est qu'une aggrégation de parties toujours trop séparées, et qui conservent toujours une tendance à se diviser, par la diversité de leurs loix, de leurs moeurs, de leurs opinions; par l'inégalité de leurs forces actuelles; plus encore par l'inégalité de leurs progrès ultérieurs.[20]

Such a state of affairs, if persisted in, could but be of ill omen for the development of a great united America of the future.

When Turgot wrote this letter, he had seen only the constitutions of New York, Massachusetts, Maryland, and the first con-

[17] *Ibid.*, p. 380.
[18] *Ibid.*, p. 382.

[19] *Ibid.*, p. 383.
[20] *Ibid.*

stitution of Pennsylvania.[21] He praised the last, because Franklin,
reputedly a follower of the physiocratic school, was believed
to be responsible for the introduction in it of the one-assembly
system.[22] But his violent attack upon the other three, implied in
his letter and made known in 1784, when it was published in the
appendix to Price's pamphlet *Observations on the Importance of
the American Revolution*, aroused John Adams to a celebrated
defense of the American Constitution.

The three volumes of John Adams' *Defense of the Constitutions
of Government of the U. S. of America*, published in 1787–88,
were written in answer to a letter of less than twenty pages. But
Turgot's attack had not been without consequences even in Boston,
and Adams had had much to do with the Massachusetts constitution.[23] His answer "cost" him three volumes, as he says, but the
results were good enough to justify all his labors among "Italian
ruins and rubbish." [24]

Adams' only purpose was to write a defense of "the distribution of the legislative power into three branches, in separating the
executive from the legislative power, and the judiciary power from
both," and to refute Turgot's principal thesis of the necessity
for a concentration of power.[25] The fact that English customs
had been followed by some of the American constitutions was no
proof of their inherent evil.

> If those customs were wise, just and good, and calculated to secure the liberty,
> property and safety of the people, as well, or better, than any other institutions,
> ancient or modern, would M. Turgot have advised the nation to reject them, merely
> because it was at that time justly incensed against the English Parliament?

The truth is that the principle of the separation of powers had
not been adopted as an imitation of what England had done, but
because "it was founded in nature and reason," a foundation lack-

[21] Cf. Adams to Taylor, April 1814, *Works of John Adams*, edited by Charles F.
Adams (Boston, 1851–56), VI, 486.

[22] Cf. Adams to Perley, Quincy, June 19, 1809, *Works*, IX, 622–623. Adams,
however, denies that Franklin had anything to do with the Pennsylvania constitution.

[23] "In 1780, when I arrived in France, I carried a printed copy of the report of
the Grand Committee of the Massachusetts Convention, which I had drawn up;
and this became an object of speculation. Mr. Turgot . . . and others, admired
Mr. Franklin's Constitution and reprobated mine" (*Works*, IX, 623). Turgot's
letter, however, had been written two years earlier.

[24] Adams to Jefferson, London, August 25, 1787, *ibid*, VIII, 448.

[25] Adams to Perley, *ibid*., IX, 624; Adams to Price, New York, May 20, 1785,
ibid., IX, 558.

ing in Turgot's proposal of "collecting all authority into one center," especially when that center was to be, in Turgot's words, the nation.[26] Adams clearly saw that it was not possible to reconcile the despotism which a centralization of powers implies with the democracy which was presupposed by the stressing of the concept of nation.

2. THE ISSUE OF JUDICIAL REVIEW. STEVENS VERSUS ADAMS

The full circle of the polemic was still far from being completed with the publication of the *Defense*. Following Turgot's attack upon American constitutions as copies of the English system — the result of an uncritical acceptance of Montesquieu's traditional picture of the British constitution, — and Adams' answer, which was a defense of the separation of powers but not necessarily of English institutions, John Stevens took Adams to task because he had failed to see that the system of separation had led in England to the supremacy of the legislative branch over the other branches of government, thus nullifying all attempts to achieve a balance of power.

The famous American engineer, whose work appeared in 1789 in a French edition,[27] was bitterly critical of the so-called English constitution and of the system of checks and balances so highly praised by Adams.

C'est en vain que les Anglois se vantent d'avoir une constitution, puisque l'on chercheroit en vain dans leurs anciens registres un pacte original. Chez eux, aucune partie du gouvernement ne peut être regardée comme fixée ou comme établie d'une manière inaltérable. Il n'existe aucune barrière, aucun frein au pouvoir du parle-

---

[26] *Defense, ibid.,* IV, 300, 301.
[27] *Examen du gouvernement d'Angleterre comparé aux constitutions des Etats-Unis.* The *Examen* covers pp. 1–66, the notes pp. 67–287. In the *Avertissement,* the authorship is explicitly credited to William Livingston, Governor of New Jersey (pp. v–vi). The original American edition appeared in New York in 1787, under the title *Observations on Government; including some animadversions on Mr. Adams' Defense of the Constitution of Government of the United States, and Mr. De Lolme's Constitution of England,* by A Farmer of New Jersey. The pamphlet was, at the time, universally accepted as coming from Livingston's pen. Together with all catalogues of American libraries, Sabin's *Bibliotheca Americana* attributed it to Livingston (1878, vol. X, p. 411), and a correction was only recently made (1932–33, vol. XXIII, p. 420) following the publication of A. D. Turnbull, *John Stevens, an American record* (New York, 1928), where definite proof is offered of John Stevens' authorship (cf. pp. 90–91). Jefferson, however, was never in doubt, for, on the front page of his copy of the now exceedingly rare (and not available for the present study) American edition of the pamphlet, he wrote "John Stevens of N. Jersey" (Jefferson Collection, Library of Congress).

ment. Il est, dans le langage de leurs publicistes, *tout puissant*, et c'est, je crois, une idée de Locke, qu'il peut tout faire, excepté de changer un homme en femme.[28]

Did Adams foresee the possibility of a dictatorship of the legislative branch? Apparently yes, and with approval. Such an outcome, Stevens believes, is not to be avoided in those countries where the legislative power "est concentré dans une seule assemblée de représentans, sans qu'on ait pris la précaution de placer aucun frein dans les mains du pouvoir exécutif ou du pouvoir judiciaire." [29] Some of the American states are leaning dangerously in that direction, and some provision against this tendency will have to be taken, if the Constitution is to have any meaning at all:

Quoique nos gouvernemens ne soient en activité que depuis fort peu de temps, cependant plusieurs corps législatifs ont été saisis de cette soif du pouvoir si dangereuse. En conséquence, il est indispensable d'accorder un droit de négative aux pouvoirs exécutif et judiciaire, afin qu'ils puissent être en état de se défendre des entreprises de la puissance législative. Toutes les fois que ce frein manque, la constitution doit nécessairement être flottante et mal assûrée. Par la suite, l'expérience convaincra le peuple du besoin de ce remède, et nous avons tout lieu d'espérer qu'enfin il deviendra une loi fondamentale dans la constitution de chaque état de la confédération.[30]

Despite this defect, how much better already is the American legislative system than the British, he says, having in mind "les barrières puissantes qu'on a opposées aux entreprises du pouvoir législatif." [31]

Stevens concludes his interesting remarks on the necessity of a judicial or executive check on the mischievous activities of an all-powerful assembly (and we have reproduced them at some length because they do not appear to be widely known) with a concrete proposal of amendment to the Federal Constitution which had just then been agreed upon at Philadelphia. The president, the chief justice of the Supreme Court, and the secretary of the treasury should have jointly "un pouvoir de révision de tous les bills qui auront été approuvés par la Chambre des Représentans et par le Sénat." [32]

It was precisely this proposal to limit the extent of legislative powers that caused, as we have seen,[33] a very critical comment by Dupont, who, having relinquished his former stand in favor

---

[28] *Examen*, pp. 45–46.
[29] *Ibid.*, p. 59.
[30] *Ibid.*, p. 59.

[31] *Ibid.*, pp. 60–61.
[32] *Ibid.*, p. 62.
[33] Cf. above, p. 62.

of judicial control, and not noticing the danger which it represented if the still cherished rigid constitutional frame was to be preserved, was now in favor of the supremacy of the legislative branch. The debate was now closed during which marked contrasts between the American writers and the followers of Quesnay had come to the surface. The two physiocrats, Turgot and Dupont, had taken a common stand, a stand which was, however, the basis of a spirited attack against English institutions by Turgot and of an equally spirited defense of their underlying principles by Dupont.

3. JEFFERSON AND DUPONT

Several years later, Dupont was still expressing his doubts of the practical working of the American doctrine of separation of powers. It would be necessary, Dupont adds, to wait some time before passing final judgment, and in the meantime it must be remembered that the American Constitution had not been approved by Franklin, Madison, Livingston, or Jefferson.[34]

Jefferson's name, used by Dupont in support of his thesis, should not betray anybody into believing that conformity of opinion existed between the two. Rather, many and deep-seated were the motives of contrast in the political sphere, as we are today fully able to appreciate, thanks to the enterprise of Gilbert Chinard.[35]

These differences in temperament and doctrine [writes Chinard] are strikingly conspicuous in the correspondence between the founder of *Physiocratie* and the father of American democracy. For more than seventeen years they discussed in their letters every possible subject relating to government. . . . There will appear the contrast between two entirely different conceptions of democratic or representative government. . . . It will be seen in these letters how two men who esteemed, respected and even admired each other, experienced at times almost insuperable difficulties in understanding and penetrating one another's mind.[36]

[34] *Constitution pour la République française* (Paris, 1795), pp. 86–87, note 3. In 1788 Franklin had thanked Dupont for sending him useful suggestions: "It is probable . . . that, at the first meeting of the New Congress, various amendments will be proposed and discussed, when I hope your *Ouvrage sur les principes et le bien des républiques en général*, etc., may be ready to put into their hands, and such a work from your hand, I am confident, though it may not be entirely followed, will afford useful hints, and produce advantages of importance" (Franklin to Dupont [Philadelphia, June 9, 1788], *Writings*, IX, 658–659). Dupont's essay does not appear to have ever been published either in French or in English. Schelle merely quotes Franklin's letter (*Du Pont*, p. 271).

[35] See *The Correspondence of Jefferson and Du Pont de Nemours*.

[36] "Introduction," *Correspondence*, p. xiii. This interpretation seems to me correct. At the same time it does not perhaps entirely agree with Chinard's own

A good instance of such opposed ideals is to be found in Dupont's treatment of certain fundamental issues in his project of a constitution for the South American republics, which was prepared in the years 1815 and 1816 but of which today nothing more is known than the reaction it aroused in Jefferson. Dupont, ever faithful on this point to the physiocratic doctrine, had created the two categories of *citoyens* and *habitans*, the former including the landowners admitted to the enjoyment of all political rights, the latter made up of the landless classes.

To them, that is to say, to the industrial workers and day-laborers, Dupont admitted that society owes protection: they were entitled to the enjoyment of their personal property, to free speech, freedom of religion, habeas corpus and such natural rights. But he energetically denied that they should participate in the government of the country. . . . Thus the natural right which gives every person the faculty of expressing one's ideas on any subject viva voce or in writing, does not include the power of deliberating and of voting on other people's affairs.[37]

To any such distinction Jefferson was of course opposed, as well as to any complicated proposal of indirect democracy. Jefferson writes:

Your three or four alambications have indeed a seducing appearance. We should conceive prima facie, that the last extract would be the pure alcohol of the substance, three or four times rectified; but in proportion as they are more and more sublimated, they are also farther and farther removed from the controul of society, and human character, we believe, requires in general constant and immediate controul to prevent its being biassed from right by the seductions of self love. Your process produces, therefore, a structure of government from which the fundamental principle of ours is excluded. You first set as zeros all individuals not having lands, which are the greater number in any society of long standing. . . . I acknowledge myself strong affection for our own form. Yet both of us act and think from the same motive. We both consider the people as our children, and love them with parental affection. But you love them as infants whom you are afraid to trust without nurses, and I as adults, whom I freely leave to self government.[38]

These words would appear to leave no doubts of the nature of the dissension separating Dupont and Jefferson, although the men were united by a close friendship which extended over a period of more than thirty years and which doctrinal differences never weakened.

---

subsequent words to the effect that whatever differences there existed between Dupont and Jefferson were owing merely to "circumstances and their individual temperaments" (*Ibid.*, p. cxxiii).

[37] *Ibid.*, p. lxvi.

[38] Jefferson to Dupont, Poplar Forest, April 24, 1816, *Correspondence*, pp. 257–258.

Dupont had always aimed at creating a pleasant exchange of ideas between the physiocratic school and America. As editor of the *Ephémérides* he was responsible for the publication or discussion in the journal of writings of Franklin,[39] John Dickinson,[40] and Mansword;[41] and he had succeeded in winning Franklin's approval of the school's doctrines: "There is such a freedom from local and national prejudices and partialities, so much benevolence to mankind in general, so much goodness mixt with wisdom, in the principles of your new philosophy, that I am perfectly charmed with them." [42]

Later, Dupont was to make himself useful to American interests.[43] Jefferson, who had thus become personally acquainted with Dupont, was so pleased and struck by Dupont's ability that he subsequently never tired of recommending his writings to his

[39] The list of writings by Franklin which appeared in the *Ephémérides* follows (with the English title and reference to the Smyth edition of Franklin's works given in parenthesis):

(a) "Lettre d'un Fermier au Public Anglois, sur les terreurs et les soulevements populaires qu'a occasionnés la cherté des pains; et sur les moyens qu'on a pris pour y remédier" (1767), II, 8–18. (*"On the Price of Corn, and Management of the Poor,"* V, 334–339.) The letter had been taken from the *London Chronicle*, where it had been published in November 1766.

(b) "Des troubles qui divisent l'Angleterre et ses colonies" (1768), VII, 28–91; VIII, 159–192. ("Examination of Dr. B. Franklin in the British House of Commons," IV, 412–448.) In an introduction, Dupont praises Franklin's understanding of the new philosophy: "Accoutumé dès l'enfance à saisir la vérité dans toutes les études auxquelles il [Franklin] s'est livré, ce sage Amériquain a été frappé, dès qu'on lui en a parlé, de l'enchainement de celles qui depuis quelques années réduisent ce qu'on a nommé l'art de gouverner les Nations, à une science exacte. Il est devenu rapidement un des plus habiles adeptes de cette Science sublime, qui éprouve encore, dans le pays où elle a pris naissance, des contradictions par lesquelles ses progrès ne sont point retardés, et dont ses Défenseurs se consolent aisément, par le plaisir de faire quelques conquêtes du poids et du mérite de celle de M. Franklin" (pp. 32–33). Cf. also above, p. 75.

(c) "Positions à examiner" (1769), X, 5–16. ("Positions to be Examined, Concerning National Wealth," V, 200–202.) This article was translated from the *London Chronicle* of June 29, 1769.

(d) "Projet pour un voyage à la Nouvelle Zeelande" (1772), II, 213–224. ("Plan for Benefiting Distant Countries," V, 340–344.)

[40] The *Lettres d'un fermier de Pensylvanie aux habitants de l'Amérique septentrionale par M. Dickinson*, are reviewed at length by Dupont, *Ephémérides* (1769), X, 43–121.

[41] Cf. above, pp. 75–76.

[42] Franklin to Dupont, London, July 28, 1768, *Writings*, V, 155.

[43] "Du Pont has rendered us essential services." Jefferson to Jay, Paris, Nov. 3, 1787, *The Writings of Thomas Jefferson* (New York, 1892–99, ed. P. L. Ford), V, 358.

correspondents [44] and of praising him "as the ablest man in France." [45]

It was towards the close of the century, when all hopes of democracy in France had been dashed to the ground, that Dupont felt the urge to leave his country and to settle in America [46] so as to die a free man: "Je veux mourir dans un pays où la liberté ne soit pas seulement dans les loix, toujours plus ou moins bien, plus ou moins mal exécutées, mais principalement dans les constantes habitudes de la nation." [47] Jefferson knew of Dupont's intention of starting an agricultural colony, and as soon as his friend arrived in New York he warned him against land speculators.[48] The warning was not necessary, however, since the Duponts immediately realized their lack of preparedness for any earnest colonizing project. And when the son, Eleuthère-Irénée, decided to start a powder factory in Delaware, the plans were definitely altered, with the result that Dupont had to return to France in 1802 in order to explain to the backers of the enterprise the reasons for the change.

Dupont should have stayed in France only six months, but thirteen years elapsed before he finally returned to America. The edition of Turgot's works which he had decided to undertake was the cause of the delay. In 1808 only four volumes were out:

Je vois par ce qui reste de matériaux . . . qu'il y en aura au moins trois autres — cela fini, je serai quitte envers l'ancien continent, et mes voeux, mes pas devront se tourner vers celui auquel je pourrai rendre quelque service, où la liberté pourra être durable, où mes enfants sont établis.[49]

In 1811 his labors were not yet at an end. "Je ne sais encore quand je serai libre de retourner vous voir et porter le tribut de mes

[44] "I send you a book by Du Pont on the subject of the commercial treaty with England . . . you will pick up in various parts of it such excellent principles and observations, as will richly repay the trouble of reading it." Jefferson to Madison, Paris, July 31, 1788, *Writings*, VIII, 96.

[45] Jefferson to T. M. Randolph, Philadelphia, Jan. 17, 1799, *Writings*, XVIII, 211.

[46] If John Adams had had his way, probably the Duponts would never have reached America: "I shall not be guilty of so much affectation of regard to sciences, as to be very willing to grant passports to Dupont de Nemours or any other French philosophers, in the present situation of our country. We have had too many French philosophers already, and I really begin to think, or rather to suspect, that learned academies, not under the immediate inspection and control of government, have disorganized the world and are incompatible with social order" (Adams to Pickering, Quincy, Sept. 16, 1798, *Works*, VIII, 596).

[47] Dupont to Jefferson, Paris, Aug. 27, 1798, *Correspondence*, p. 7.

[48] Jefferson to Dupont [January] 1800, *Correspondence*, p. 9.

[49] Dupont to Jefferson, Paris, May 25, 1808, *Correspondence*, p. 126.

derniers jours à vos nobles et sages citoyens qui leur sont main-
tenant l'unique espoir du monde." [50] But his impatience was
growing, and he was writing Jefferson: "Je veux être enterré en
terre sainte, c'est-à-dire enterré libre. Il me semble que j'y serai
plus tranquille." [51]

Now Jefferson was urging Dupont not to risk a third crossing
of the ocean: "At your time of life, it is scarcely perhaps advisable.
An exchange of the society, the urbanity, and the real comforts
to which you have been formed by the habits of a long life, would
be a great and real sacrifice." [52]

It was, however, impossible to check the youthful enthusiasm
of Dupont, who in May 1815 landed again in New York. He was
now seventy-six, but he wrote Madison he was going to give every
ounce of his strength to the new country: "J'espère avoir dix ans
à lui donner. Si elle a par hazard besoin de mon travail et de ma
plume, elle aura ma plume et mon travail. Si elle avait besoin de
mon sang, j'en ai encore dans les veines, elle aurait mon sang." [53]
His last words to Jefferson were: "Mon ami, nous sommes des
limaçons, et nous avons à monter sur les Cordillières. *Par dieu*
il y faut monter." [54]

4. The American and Physiocratic Doctrines of Judicial Control

The preceding pages on physiocracy and America have revealed
controversy and opposition rather than concurrence in the ideals
of government. With America evolving at the same time a doc-

---

[50] Dupont to Jefferson, Paris, March 31, 1811, *Correspondence*, p. 162.

[51] Dupont to Jefferson, Paris, July 4, 1811, *Correspondence*, p. 168.

[52] Jefferson to Dupont, Monticello, Nov. 29, 1813, *Correspondence*, pp. 208–209.

[53] Dupont to Madison, New York, May 1815, *Correspondence*, p. 221.

[54] Dupont to Jefferson, August 18, 1816, *Correspondence*, p. 273. Dupont died
on August 7, 1817. The importance of Dupont's rôle in the history of the Louisiana
purchase is revealed by his correspondence with Jefferson (cf. "Introduction,"
pp. xxvii-xliv). Significant, too, as representing a departure from the traditional
physiocratic doctrine, is his defense of an industrial development of the United
States (cf. "Sur l'agriculture et les Manufactures aux Etats-Unis," a memorandum
addressed to Madison on January 18, 1816 [*Correspondence*, pp. 240–250]). Jefferson sought Dupont's advice on matters of education, and on the courses of study
to be given at the University of Virginia. Cf. Jefferson to Dupont, Philadelphia,
April 12, 1800, *Correspondence*, pp. 11–12; and Dupont, *Sur l'éducation nationale
dans les Etats-Unis d'Amérique* (Paris, 1812, but written in 1800), with which the
name of the Chevalier Quesnay de Beaurepaire, grandson of the founder of the
physiocratic school, is also connected. Cf. Herbert B. Adams, *Jefferson and the
University of Virginia* (Washington, 1888), pp. 22 ff.; and Philip A. Bruce, *History
of the University of Virginia* (New York, 1920–22), I, 55 ff.

trine of judicial control similar to that of the physiocrats, no evidence is to be found that the former owes anything to the latter. Of the physiocratic doctrine one phase had especially struck the American mind, the advocacy of a unified system of government, with all legislative and executive power in the hands of the sovereign. Nothing would have been better calculated to alienate American sympathies than a doctrine which so completely struck at the conception of the separation of powers, then, and ever since, dear to the American people.[55] But nothing also was further removed from the real picture than such a partial interpretation of the physiocratic political doctrine. Yet it probably influenced Benjamin Franklin in its stand for a concentration of powers.[56]

The physiocratic doctrine of judicial control, lost in France under the verbose polemics aroused by other, more easily grasped, economic and political aspects of the school's teachings, escaped the attention of American theorists. Of it we find no trace among the writings of the advocates of the parallel American doctrine. The usually thankless investigation of relative influences and derivations cannot happily be pursued in this case.

What matters is that the American doctrine of judicial control owes its existence to essentially the same principle that stimulated the physiocrats in their search for a permanent and stable solution of the problems of government, that is, the belief in the existence of a higher order to be preserved against the inroads of legislators, who must in consequence be allowed definitely restricted powers.

The conditions under which the American experiment of securing the recognition of this higher order of laws of nature was attempted, were favorable. They were favorable

not only to the reception of higher law theories but also to their incorporation as basic doctrines of public and private law. . . . The judges in the Colonies frequently indicated their belief in the natural laws, which were considered true laws, and legislation was thought to be binding only in so far as it was an expression of these laws.[57]

[55] Cf. B. F. Wright, Jr., "The Origins of the Separation of Powers in America," *Economica*, XIII (1933), 169 ff.

[56] Malcolm R. Eiselen, *Franklin's Political Theories* (New York, 1928). On the influence of the economic doctrine of the physiocrats on Franklin, see Lewis J. Carey, *Franklin's Economic Views* (New York, 1928), chap. VII.

[57] Charles G. Haines, *The Revival of Natural Law Concepts* (Cambridge, 1930), pp. 52–53.

Positive law was but "a reflection of an ideal body of perfect rules demonstrable by reason, and valid for all times, all places and all men. Positive legal precepts got their validity from their conformity to these ideals." [58] When this ideal body of rules was translated into written constitutions, the reverence given the former was granted to the latter, and the courts, which had for a long time acted as interpreters of the precepts of natural laws and as defenders of human rights against the encroachments of legislators and rulers, came to be generally and immediately accepted as the true expounders of the law, the body in whom resided the power of declaring what the true law was.

The grant of the power of review to the courts in the physiocratic state was more explicit, and the courts had been set up openly as constitutional courts. Procedural methods were thus different from those which were to be followed in the United States. But this merely stresses the identity of the motives and purposes behind the institution of judicial control. One finds the same distrust towards legislators; the same belief that essentially all rules of human conduct are written by the divine hand and are there for the ruler to interpret and to follow; the same desire, therefore, to limit legislative activities, to have a body of interpreters of these rules of natural law for the protection of individual rights, including those property rights which were considered by the physiocrats as pre-social.[59]

But while conditions in the United States had been favorable to the reception of the doctrines of higher law and of the judges as its interpreters, the difficulties which the physiocratic doctrine had to meet in France were not small. There was the skepticism with which the doctrine was received, coming as it did from a school that had identified itself with the call for a legal despot. The sincerity of the physiocrats' protestations that they really meant to invest the judiciary with supreme powers of control over the despot was doubted. Yet, as has been said elsewhere in this monograph, the substance of the physiocratic claim and the reality of their doctrine of judicial control cannot be questioned. It

[58] Roscoe Pound, "The Theory of Judicial Decision," *Harvard Law Review*, XXXVI (1923), 802.

[59] "The French Physiocrats . . . are especially emphatic in proclaiming the origin of private property in the state of nature, and the duty of the state to recognize it in virtue of *les lois naturelles de l'ordre social*" (Gierke, *Natural Law and the Theory of Society, 1500–1800*, II, 294).

was left to later generations to recognize the balance of their political system; but this recognition would have come earlier, had the necessary favorable circumstances been present.

Two were, however, the chief adverse factors. One we have identified in the tradition of the parliaments. This may appear, on the surface, to be strange. But as we have attempted to demonstrate elsewhere, notwithstanding the great number of theoretical claims to an effective and ultimate power of control upon royal acts — claims, be it noted, mostly advanced outside of the parliaments — the parliaments had come to accept their subordinate position, leaving the royal power triumphant. When the physiocrats came upon the scene there was not the slightest doubt that parliament had definitely lost on the issue of control of legislative acts. And any attempt, therefore, to revitalize the issue of judicial control under the aegis of the very body that had been defeated in its struggle for supremacy was doomed to failure.

Just as the physiocratic doctrine met opposition in its own period, so it did later, when Rousseau's notion of the general will was accepted. The basic premise of the doctrine of judicial control that there was a distinction between a higher order of fundamental laws and a lower order of men-made laws was extraneous to Rousseau's thought. Every law was valid which had received the approval of the people, following the accepted procedure, whatever the content of it may be. To the physiocrats law was not *the* expression of will of the sovereign, but only *that* expression of the will of the sovereign which answered certain essential principles and was compatible with them. It was impossible to reconcile the two opposing systems,[60] and it was not the physiocratic which prevailed in the years that followed.[61]

[60] Rousseau had been pungently satirical at the expense of the physiocrats; the legal despot aroused his ire, together with the abstractness of Le Mercier's *Ordre*. "Je n'ai jamais pu bien entendre ce que c'était que cette évidence qui sert de base au *despotisme légal*. . . . Il me semble que l'évidence ne peut jamais être dans les lois naturelles et politiques qu'en les considérant par abstraction. Dans un gouvernement particulier, que tant d'éléments divers composent, cette évidence disparaît nécessairement. Car la science du gouvernement n'est qu'une science de combinaisons, d'applications et d'exceptions, selon les temps, les lieux, les circonstances. . . . Messieurs, permettez-moi de vous le dire, vous donnez trop de force à vos calculs, et pas assez aux penchants du coeur humain et au jeu des passions. Votre système est très bon pour les gens de l'Utopie; il ne vaut rien pour les enfants d'Adam" (Rousseau to Mirabeau [Trye, July 26, 1767], *Political Writings of J. J. Rousseau*, ed. Vaughan [Cambridge, 1915], II, 159–160).

[61] For a summary of the issue of the control of legislative acts in France at the end of the eighteenth and at the beginning of the nineteenth centuries, cf. my *Origini dottrinali e storiche della dottrina del controllo giudiziario sulla costituzionalità delle leggi negli Stati Uniti* (Turin, 1930), Introduction, pp. 13 ff.

INDEX

INDEX

Adams, H. B., 87
Adams, John, 75; his answer to Turgot in defense of the separation of powers, 80–81; criticized by Stevens, 81; attacks Dupont, 86
Agriculture, and the physiocratic economic system, 10 ff., 44; and Cantillon, 10–11; Quesnay's view of, 11
Ameline, Léon, 7, 8
America, and the problem of its independence in physiocratic thought, 73 ff.; its constitutional problems as viewed by the physiocrats, 75; growing contrasts between the American and the physiocratic conceptions of government, 76 ff.; and the acceptance of the laws of nature, 88

Barbier, Antoine, 17
Barker, Ernest, 3
Baudeau, Nicolas, 3, 14, 15, 16; answers Béardé, 71–72
Baudrillart, Henri, 7
Béardé de l'Abbaye, 69; and the power of the courts, 71–72
Bibliotheca Americana, 81
Blondel, André, 5
Bonar, James, 3, 7
Bruce, Philip A., 87
Butré, Charles de, his life and contributions to the doctrine of judicial control, 18; 29; his defense of judicial control against Mably, 37; 67

Cantillon, Richard, and agriculture, 10–11
Carey, Lewis J., 88
Carl Friedrich von Baden, 18
Carl Ludwig von Baden, 59
Charles IX, 48
Cheinisse, Léon, 4, 6, 7, 8, 31
China, held up as example by Quesnay, 31; and the supremacy of the courts, 66, 67
Chinard, Gilbert, 83
Coquille, Guy de, and the theoretical rights of the *parlements*, 49

Daire, Eugène, 15
Dickinson, John, 85
Doolin, Paul Rice, 50
Dupont de Nemours, Pierre Samuel, 9, 12, 13; his contribution to the doctrine of judicial control, 15–16; Le Mercier's influence, 15; 18; and natural order, 21; his summary of physiocratic doctrine, 25–26, 29; and Quesnay, 32; theory of legislation and judicial control, 44 ff., 52; his abandonment of judicial control, 59 ff.; his activity as member of the Constituent Assembly and of the *Conseil des Anciens*, 63–65, 66, 71, 72; and the independence of America, 73; and Franklin, 75; 82; and Jefferson, 83 ff.; his distinction between *citoyen* and *habitant* opposed by Jefferson, 84; settles in America, 86; his edition of Turgot's works, 86–87; his death, 87

Einaudi, Luigi, 12, 23
Eiselen, Malcolm R., 88
Ephémérides du citoyen, 13, 14, 16, 17, 18, 30, 32, 37, 38, 67, 68, 71, 73, 75, 85
Esmein, Adhémar, 8, 34
Etats généraux, 29

Fayard, Ennamond, 51
Flammermont, Jules, 48, 49, 50, 51
Forbonnais, François de, his hostility to the physiocrats, 69
Franklin, Benjamin, and the repeal of the Stamp Act, 73; as a disciple of the physiocrats, 75; and the constitution of Pennsylvania, 80; 83; and the *Ephémérides*, 85; and the concentration of powers, 88
French Revolution, anticipated by physiocrats, 3; and Le Mercier's constitutionalism, 53 ff.; and its influence upon Dupont's abandonment of judicial control, 59 ff.

Galiani, Ferdinando, his attack against the physiocrats, 14

Gierke, Otto, 3, 89

Girard, René, 4

Glasson, Ernest, 51

Gournay, Vincent de, 43

Grand Conseil, 48, 50

Graslin, Jean Joseph, 72

Güntzberg, Benedikt, 8

Gurvitch, Georges, 22, 23

Haines, Charles G., 88

Hasbach, Wilhelm, 7

Higgs, Henry, 7, 10, 11, 69

Hobbes, Thomas, 63

Hübner, Martin, 67

Individualism, and Le Trosne's conception of the state, 4; and society, 21; and Dupont, 63; and Mirabeau, 77

International order, its description by Le Trosne, 35

Isambert, François, 48, 49

Janet, Paul, and the judicial guarantee, 5

Jefferson, Thomas, 44, 65, 75; and John Stevens, 81; and Dupont, 83 ff.; opposed to Dupont's indirect democracy, 84; his praise of Dupont, 85–86; and the University of Virginia, 87

Journal de l'Agriculture, du Commerce et des Finances, 13

Judicial control, as part of the physiocratic doctrine, 7 ff.; physiocratic and American doctrines, 8; real extension of physiocratic doctrine, 9; physiocratic sources, chap. III; accepted by Le Trosne, 36–37; by Butré, 37–38; by La Vauguyon, 39–40; by Le Mercier, 41 ff.; by Dupont, 44–46; and the *parlements*, 47 ff.; as part of a constitutional system, 53 ff.; abandoned by Dupont, 59 ff.; its early general acceptance by the school, 67–68; contemporary critics, 69 ff.; favored by Mansword for America, 76; its advocacy by Stevens, 82; a parallel between the physiocratic and the American doctrines, 87 ff.; obstacles in its way in France, 89–90

Judicial power, as a defense of natural laws, 5, 6; crowning feature of phys-iocratic state, 28; in China, 31; descriptions of its duties by La Vauguyon, 38–40; its role according to Le Mercier, 40 ff.; and to Dupont, 45–46; its role in Le Mercier's constitutional system, 55–56; and Mably, 69–70; and Béardé de l'Abbaye, 71; in the United States, 89

Kellner, G., 7

Lardier, Joseph, 17

Laski, Harold J., 20

La Vauguyon, Paul François de, his contribution to the doctrine of judicial control, 16–17; his life, 17; 29; defense against Mably of the courts' power of control, 38–40; influenced by Le Mercier, 40; 66, 67

Lavergne, Léonce de, 4, 5, 7, 27

Law, administrative, distinguished from constitutional, 54, 57, 58

———, constitutional, as a safeguard of the physiocratic order, 36; its treatment by Le Mercier, 54 ff.; 89

———, natural, basis of system of guarantees, 4; its defense, 5 ff.; in a physiocratic state, 28; its sanctity according to Quesnay, 30 ff.; highest type of law, according to Le Trosne, 35; its recognition in America, 88

———, positive, 20 ff.; test of its validity according to Le Mercier, and necessary concordance with natural order, 22; consequences of violation of the order according to Mirabeau, 23–24; its verification according to Quesnay, 30–31; emphasized by Le Trosne, 34; its formal and substantive nature according to Le Mercier, 40; 89

Legal depotism, 3; misunderstandings arising from term, 4; defenses against, 5 ff.; a consequence of Quesnay's *Tableau économique*, 10; and natural order, 27 ff.; as interpreted by La Vauguyon, 39; Dupont's new phrasing, 44

Legislative power, limited according to Le Trosne, 35; God the only legislator, 36; relationship with judicial power, 42–43; and the *parlements*, 48; and Le Mercier's constitution, 57; new scope given to it by Dupont, 61–62;

its dictatorship feared by Stevens, 82

Le Gros, Abbé, 14, 69

Leibnitz, Gottfried Wilhelm, 22

Le Mercier de la Rivière, Pierre François, 9, 13; his contribution to the doctrine of judicial control, 14–15; 17, 18; his distinction between natural and positive law, 21–22; 29; his influence upon Mirabeau, 33; 37; nature of positive law, 40; functions of judges, 40 ff.; 47; and the constitutional place of judicial control, 53 ff.; coherence of his thought, 58–59; 60, 66, 67; attacked by Mably, 69 ff.; 90

Lepaige, Louis Adrien, 51

Le Trosne, Guillaume François, 4, 5; his contribution to the doctrine of judicial control, 18–19; 29; his mitigation of legal despotism, 34; his three types of law, 35–36; and judicial control, 36–37; 67; his admiration for the American people, 74–75

Linguet, Simon Nicolas, 72

Lit de justice, nullifies parliamentary control, 47, 51; and the validity of royal edicts, 50

Livingston, William, his alleged authorship of Stevens' pamphlet, 81; 83

Locke, John, 82

Loménie, Louis Léonard de, 30

Lorion, André, 8

Loyseau, Charles, 49

Mably, Gabriel Bonnot de, 17, 18, 37; and La Vauguyon, 38; 66, 67; his attacks on the physiocrats, 69 ff.

McIlwain, Charles H., 48

Madison, John, 83, 87

Mallet du Pan, Jacques, 53

Mansword, Abraham, and his letters in the Pennsylvania Chronicle, 75–76; 85

Martin, Kingsley, 50

Mazarin, Jules, 50

Mazzei, Filippo, 77

Michel, Henri, 3, 7

Mille, Jérôme, 35

Mirabeau, Victor Riquetti, Marquis de, 13; his contribution to the doctrine of judicial control, 14; 17, 18; his view of the reasons for society's decay, 23–24, 28; 29; his collaboration with Quesnay, 30; his doctrine of the legal order, 32–34; 43, 66; his remarks on the Virginia Declaration of Rights, 76–77

Monarchy, as a basis of the physiocratic state, 3; limited according to Quesnay, 6, 29; 45; and the parlements, 49 ff.

Montesquieu, Charles Secondat, Baron de, 23; criticized by Dupont, 43; 81

Moreau, Jacob Nicolas, censor of the Ephémérides, 68

Nouvelles Ephémérides économiques, 15

Oncken, August, 4, 7, 13

Order, natural, physiocratic conception, 20 ff.; its superior validity for Le Mercier, 42

Ordonnance, as distinguished from loi, according to Quesnay, 32

Parlements, and the doctrine of judicial control, 47 ff.; and Le Mercier, 56; disliked by Dupont, 59; as an obstacle to judicial control, 90

Pennsylvania, and the religious oath, 78; its constitution praised by Turgot, 80

Pennsylvania Chronicle, 75

Petiet, 48, 49, 50

Petzet, Wolfgang, 7, 8, 27

Physiocrats, significance of their political doctrines debated, 3 ff.; economic doctrines, 10 ff.; conception of natural order, 20 ff.; creation of economic science, 25–26; and royal power, 27 ff.; and the parlements, 47 ff.; the failure of Turgot's program, 51–52; and Le Mercier's constitutionalism, 53 ff.; the impact of the French revolution on Dupont, 59 ff.; the spread of the doctrine of judicial control within the school, 66 ff.; and the independence of America, 73 ff.; contrasts with American political thought, 77 ff.; the failure of their ideal of government, 89–90

Pound, Roscoe, 89

Price, Richard, 77, 78, 80

Produit net, 11

Property, denied in America as basis of political rights, 78

Public opinion, and defense of natural order, 5, 6, 36; its force doubted by Butré, 37

Quérard, Joseph Marie, 17

Quesnay, François, 5; and monarchy, 6; his economic discovery, 10 ff.; his contributions to the doctrine of judicial control, 13; 15, 16, 18, 19; and natural rights, 21; 25, 27; and positive laws, 29 ff.; his collaboration with Le Mercier, 30; 38, 43, 44, 47, 66, 67, 75, 83

Quesnay de Beaurepaire, and the University of Virginia, 87

Raynal, Abbé Guillaume, 3

Reuss, Rodolphe, 18

Rights, individual and property, 4; natural rights and the positive order, 21; the declaration of rights and legislation, 60; the historical rights of the American colonies, 74; rights and duties, according to Mirabeau, 77

Roubaud, Pierre Joseph, and the balance of power on the American continent, 74

Rousseau, Jean Jacques, attacked by Dupont, 63; opposition of his doctrine to physiocratic thought, 90

Say, Jean Baptiste, 12, 63

Schelle, Gustave, 4, 5, 6, 7, 8, 27, 44, 60, 62, 63, 83

Schumpeter, Josef, 26

Separation of powers, attacked by Turgot, 79–80; defended by John Adams, 80–81; consequences feared by Stevens, 81–82; 88

Silberstein, Lotte, 7

Smith, Adam, 25

Socialism, and physiocracy, 3

Society, and the enjoyment of natural rights, 21; reasons of its decay according to Mirabeau, 23–24; according to Le Trosne, 34–35; and the Declaration of Rights, 61

State, limits to its authority, 6; and society, 23; causes of its ruin, 23–24; and the physiocratic sovereign, 28; Turgot's conception, 78–80

Stevens, John, 16, 60; his limitation of legislative powers criticized by Dupont, 62; views regarding supremacy of legislative branch, 81–82

Supreme Court of the United States, compared to physiocratic judges, 8

Taxation, physiocratic system, 11–12; and tyranny, 23; and violation of natural order, 26; Le Trosne's advice to America, 75

Teyssendier de la Serve, Pierre, 18

Tocqueville, Alexis de, on parallelism of physiocracy and socialism, 3; 4; and public opinion, 5; 7; and royal power, 27

Tourneux, Maurice, 49

Turgot, Anne Robert, 34, 44, 50; failure of his governmental program, 51–52; 59, 63; and the independence of America, 73–74; and his criticism of the American constitutions, 77 ff.; 83

Turnbull, A. D., 81

Voltaire, 69

Weulersse, Georges, 4, 6, 7, 8, 9, 13, 29, 76

Wright, Benjamin F., Jr., 88